# HMS VICTORY
# POCKET MANUAL
# 1805

## ADMIRAL NELSON'S FLAGSHIP AT TRAFALGAR

Peter Goodwin

OSPREY
PUBLISHING

*To Katy, Mhairi, Darcy and Mara*

This edition first published in Great Britain in 2017 by Osprey Publishing,
PO Box 883, Oxford, OX1 9PL, UK
1385 Broadway, 5th Floor, New York, NY 10018, USA
Email: info@ospreypublishing.com

Osprey Publishing is part of Bloomsbury Publishing Plc

First published by Conway 2015
© Peter Goodwin, 2015

A CIP record for this book is available from the British Library.

ISBN: 978-1-4728-3406-5
ePub ISBN: 978-1-4728-3407-2
ePDF ISBN: 978-1-4728-3404-1
XML ISBN: 978-1-4728-3405-8

Designed by CE Marketing
Printed and bound in Great Britain by CPI Group (UK) Ltd, Croydon CR0 4YY

17 18 19 20 21   10 9 8 7 6 5 4 3 2 1

**Acknowledgements**
Illustrations by Peter Goodwin, except for the endpapers: front photo by
William Collingwood Smith/Fine Art Photographic/Getty Images; back photo
by Prism/UIG via Getty Images.

**The Woodland Trust**
Osprey Publishing supports the Woodland Trust, the UK's leading woodland
conservation charity. Between 2014 and 2018 our donations are being spent on
their Centenary Woods project in the UK.

**www.ospreypublishing.com**

# CONTENTS

## APPENDICES

# INTRODUCTION

*'Heart of Oak are our Ships, Jolly tars are our men'*

*Aye stout were her timbers and stoutly commanded,*
*In the Annals of glory unchalleng'd her name,*
*Aye ready for battle when duty demanded,*
*Aye ready to conquer or die in her fame*

WORDS BY DAVID GARRICK, (ENGLISH ACTOR, 1717–1779)
MUSIC BY WILLIAM BOYCE, 1759

Launched 250 years ago, the 100-gun first-rate ship HMS *Victory*, now preserved at the historic dockyard in Portsmouth, England, is perhaps the most iconic surviving vessel of Britain's powerful Georgian Navy in the 'Age of the Fighting Sail'. More than this, the *Victory* conjures up the names of formidable Royal Naval admirals: Anson, Collingwood, Hawke, Hood, Howe, Jervis and Keppel, together with the immortal Horatio Lord Nelson. Line of battle ships like the *Victory* were formidable fighting machines: her massed firepower of 1,704lb (0.76 tons) was 35 per cent greater than that Field Marshall Wellington had available at the Battle Waterloo against the French on 18 June 1815.

From an international perspective HMS *Victory* is equally important as she alone stands testament to the classic warships of the naval powers of her era: French, Spanish, Danish, Dutch, Neapolitan, Russian, Swedish and Turkish alike. Bowing in *Victory's* wake are Britain's two other preserved 'wooden walls', the fifth-rate 46-gun frigates HMS *Trincomalee* at Hartlepool and HMS *Unicorn* in Dundee. These lesser-gunned but swifter vessels conjure up the illustrious 'frigate captains': Blackwood, Broke, Cochrane and Hoste, to name but a few. Collectively all three ships equally turn our minds to the names of fictitious heroes such as Aubrey, Bolitho, Hornblower, Ramage and Kydd created by the writers O'Brian, Kent, Forester, Pope, and Stockwin respectively.

The prefix HMS preceding the ship's name is an acronym for what was initially HBMS: His (Her) Britannic[k] Majesty's Ship. The first recorded use of the abbreviated form 'HMS' was referenced to the fifth-rate 36-gun frigate HMS *Phoenix* in 1789.

*Build me straight, O worthy Master!*
*Stanch and strong, a goodly vessel*
*That shall laugh at all disaster*
*And with wave and whirlwind wrestle!*
*The merchant's word*
*Delighted the Master heard*
*For his heart was in his work, and the heart*
*Giveth grace unto every Art*

'THE BUILDING OF THE SHIP' BY HENRY WADSWORTH LONGFELLOW (1807–1882)

*Giant oaks of wide expansion*
*O'er a hundred acres fell*
*All to build this noble mansion*
*Where our hearts of oak shall dwell*

WORDS BY THOMAS CAMPBELL

# 1

# BUILDING THE *VICTORY*

## A FIRST-RATE SHIP

Classified as a first-rate ship of 100 guns, the *Victory* represents the capital warship of her time, the equivalent of today's aircraft carrier or SSBN (submerged ship ballistic nuclear), submarines carrying intercontinental nuclear missiles of devastating destruction. The *Victory* had colossal strike power. Her total broadside weight of fire in 1805 was greater than the massed guns that Field Marshal Wellington had at his disposal at the Battle of Waterloo.

Expensive to build and maintain, such ships were a political statement, a 'don't mess with me', the flagship of an admiral and leader of battle fleets.

*'A First rate ship, fully equipped and under way, this being beyond doubt the most superb engine that the mind of Man has ever conceived'*

This statement by Sir Gilbert Blane (1749–1834), physician to the Royal Navy, encapsulates such ships in their entirety. The *Victory* is also classified as a 'ship of the line' or line of battle ship, one sufficiently armed with strongly constructed 'wooden bulwarks' to stand in the line of battle against the onslaught of enemy fire, (modern terms 'battleship' and 'liner' are derived from this).

The first English ship built with three continuous gun decks was the 55-gun *Prince Royal* built at Woolwich by Phineas Pett and launched in 1610. The first ship to carry 100 guns on three decks was the *Royal Sovereign* (sometimes called *Sovereign of the Seas*) built in 1637 by Phineas Pett. After this a total of twenty-two 100-gun ships were built up to 1810, around one every eight years, as the numbers were limited due to their immense cost to the Admiralty budget. Ships like the *Victory* remained the most potent weapons system afloat until they were overshadowed by the advent of steam propulsion and shell firing guns just 40 years after the Battle of Trafalgar.

## THE *VICTORY* IS ORDERED

In December 1758 the prime minister William Pitt the Elder persuaded the British Parliament to pass a bill authorising the building of 12 ships of the line, one being a first-rate ship of 100 guns. At this time Britain was again at war with France (Seven Years War, 1756–1763). Besides fighting in home waters, the Mediterranean and Europe as in previous conflicts, this war was fought on an intercontinental scale that enveloped North America, the East and the West Indies, India and the Philippines; it was in effect the true first world war.

The committal to build was a response to supplement the British fleet with more warships covering global deployment. On 13 December 1758 the Admiralty passed a copy of the bill to the Commissioner of HM Dockyard at Chatham authorising him to *'prepare to set up and build a new ship of 100 guns as soon as a dock is available for the purpose.'*

## DESIGNING THE *VICTORY*

The design work for the *Victory* and the other 11 ships of the building programme was undertaken by Sir Thomas Slade who was Surveyor of the Navy from 1755 until 1771. Slade was perhaps the most innovative surveyor of the eighteenth century. Prior to taking up this prestigious appointment with the Navy Board, Slade had been Assistant and then Master Shipwright at the Royal Dockyards of Woolwich and Deptford. His post as Surveyor of the Navy had been authorised by the First Lord of the Admiralty, Admiral George Anson. Between 1749 and 1769 Slade had designed 181 naval warships of varying size and purpose. Completing his plans for the yet unnamed 100-gun ship Slade submitted his designs for approval. The minutes of the Navy Board on 6 June 1759 record the following details:

*Sheer draught proposed for building the First Rate ship of 100 guns at HM Yard at Chatham pursuant to an order from the Rt. Hon. Lords Commissioners of the Admiralty 13 December last and the dimensions undermentioned viz.,*

*Length on the Gun Deck – 186 feet*

*Length of the Keel; for Tonnage – 151 feet 3 5/8 inches*

*Breath moulded – 5 feet 6 inches*

*Breadth extreme – 51 feet 10 inches*

*Burthen in tons 2162. 22/94*

*Thos.Slade*

*To carry on the Lower Deck 30 guns of 42 pounds*

*To carry on the Middle Deck 30 guns of 24 pounds*

*To carry on the Upper Deck 30 guns of 12 pounds*

*To carry on the After Deck 10 guns of 6 pounds*

*To carry on the Forecastle 2 guns of 6 pounds*

Slade's design for the *Victory* was based on the lines of captured French ships. Since the 1730s the French had applied a more scientific approach to ship design, especially with the hydrodynamic forms of the hull shape below the waterline. This particular factor was to improve sailing qualities, speed and manoeuvrability. Also copying French practice, Slade introduced a more vertical stern post on which the ship's rudder hung; this improved the manner in which a ship would answer her helm. The design of any eighteenth-century warship necessitated that it had to be fit for purpose; in the case of the *Victory* she had to function as a 'stable, manoeuvrable, floating fighting gun platform'. To achieve this Slade had to account for the following design factors:

*1. To make a Ship carry a good Sail.*

*2. To make a Ship Steer well, and quickly Answer the Helm*

*3. To make a Ship carry her Guns well out of the Water.*

*4. To make a Ship go smoothly through the Water without pitching hard*

*5. To make a Ship keep a good Wind*

*6. To have a large storage capacity allowing a ship to operate independently from base port for long periods.*

*7. To withstand the onslaught of enemy shot in order to protect the ship's own gun crews.*

On 7 July 1759 the Navy Board sent an official instruction to the officers at HM Dockyard Chatham:

> *By the Principal Officers and Commrs. of his Majys. Navy.*
> *Pursuant to the order from the Rt. Hon. the Lords Commrs. of the Admiralty dated the 13th Decr. 1758 and 14th of last month, these are to direct and require you to cause and be set up and built at your yard a new ship of 100 guns agreeable to the Draught herewith sent to you and of the Dimensions set down on the other side hereof, and you are to forthwith to prepare and send us in due form an Estimate of the Charge of Building and fitting for sea the said Ship, and providing her with Masts, Yards, Sails, Rigging and Store to an eight months' proportion. For this shall be your warrant. Dated at the Navy Office the 7th July 1759.*
> (signed)
> *Richd. Hall Tho. Slade G. Adams*
> *Th. Brett.*

The Commissioner at Chatham was Captain Thomas Cooper who had to retire in poor health the following year. The Master Shipwright who initially oversaw the *Victory's* construction was John Lock who had previously served as the Assistant Master Shipwright at Portsmouth between 1742 and 1752.

As in all times of war, royal dockyards like Chatham were working at maximum capacity with many craftsmen employed. To increase the workforce to meet the demands of the war, the Navy Board sent the following letter to all HM dockyards in February 1759: *'These are to direct you to cause all possible dispatch to be used in cleaning, refitting and storing of the ships of the line at your Port, as well as the frigates, it being of the greatest consequence that not a moment's time should be lost in getting them ready for service'.*

Chatham was no exception. In all, some 150 men were initially employed to construct the *Victory*. With the elm dock blocks laid along the axis of the Chatham's old single dock, the keel of this yet unnamed ship was laid down on Monday 23 July 1759. The site of this historic dock still exists today, although extensively modified. The dock actually lies on an east–west axis with its dock gate entering the River Medway to the west. The geographical orientation of this dock in relation to the elements and the sun would indirectly affect the construction of the ship. The occasion of laying the elm keel was witnessed by the Whig prime minister William Pitt and Admiralty representatives who had travelled down from London, after which they and the dockyard officials all attended a banquet. Much timber for the ship was available as this had been set aside 13 years earlier to build a first-rate ship 'in the room' of the fifth *Victory* which had foundered in the English Channel with all hands on 5 October, 1744.

In 1759 Britain attained a series of victories that led to a turning point in the Seven Years War, (known as the French and Indian War in North America), the French being defeated at Québec, Minden, Lagos and Quiberon Bay. As a result this year would later be known as the '*annus mirabilis*'.

## THE NAMING OF THE *VICTORY*

The decision to name the new 100-gun ship standing on the stocks at Chatham *Victory* did not come lightly, especially as her predecessor, colloquially called *Balchin's Victory,* had foundered with all hands in 1744. Despite this, she was finally named *Victory* in October 1760 and became the sixth (and last) ship in the Royal Navy to bear this name. The choice of the name was very much influenced by the events of 1759, the 'Year of Victories'. The original elaborate figurehead portrayed these events. This figure and its supports were removed during the *Victory's* 1800–03 refit and replaced with a modest, less costly figure.

| The Seven Years' War: events in 1759 | |
|---|---|
| 14 April | Battle of Bergen: French army defeats Ferdinand, Duke of Brunswick. |
| 25 July | In Canada, British forces capture Fort Niagara from French, who subsequently abandon Fort Rouillé. |
| 26 July | In North America British forces under Jeffrey Amherst capture Fort Carillon from French, and rename it Fort Ticonderoga. |
| 1 August | Battle of Minden: Anglo–Hanoverian forces under Ferdinand of Brunswick defeat the French army of the Duc de Broglie. |
| 18 August | Battle of Lagos: The British fleet of Edward Boscawen defeats a French force under Commodore Jean-François de La Clue-Sabran off the Portuguese coast. |

| 10 September | Battle of Pondicherry: An inconclusive naval battle is fought off the coast of India between the French Admiral d'Aché and the British under George Pocock. The French forces are badly damaged and sail home, never to return. |
| 13 September | Québec falls to British forces following General Wolfe's victory in the Battle of the Plains of Abraham just outside the city. Both the French Commander (the Marquis de Montcalm) and the British General James Wolfe are fatally wounded. |
| 20 November | Battle of Quiberon Bay. The British fleet of Sir Edward Hawke defeats a French fleet under Marshal de Conflans near the coast of Brittany. This is the decisive naval engagement of the Seven Years War – after this, the French are no longer able to field a significant fleet. |

Under pressure of war it was intended to complete the ship within 30 months, then quite an undertaking. When hostilities ended with the signing of the Peace of Paris on 10 February 1763 the urgency to complete the *Victory* became less critical. Consequently the workforce at Chatham was considerably reduced and laid off, leaving the dockyard with just 1325 in full employment.

Once most of the framing was complete, the ship was left to stand 'in frame' to allow the structure to settle, giving time for trimming adjustment and seasoning, the structure being temporarily retained by longitudinal battens called ribbands.

It has often been remarked that the *Victory* attained her much seasoned strength as a result of her long time standing in frame. However, while this may have been a contributory factor, in reality her time 'in frame' was governed more by events rather than practice: the Seven Years War had ended, leaving no urgency to complete the ship. The other factor was financial. The *Victory* would not be the first ship to be 'taken down' to save Parliament money.

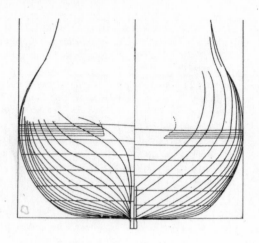

*Victory profile body plan, as built in 1765*

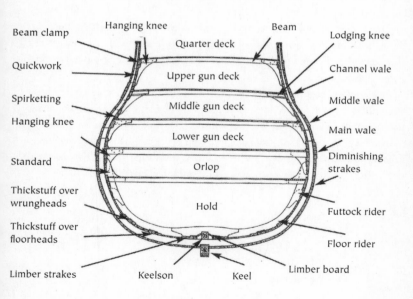

*Transverse cross-section through* Victory

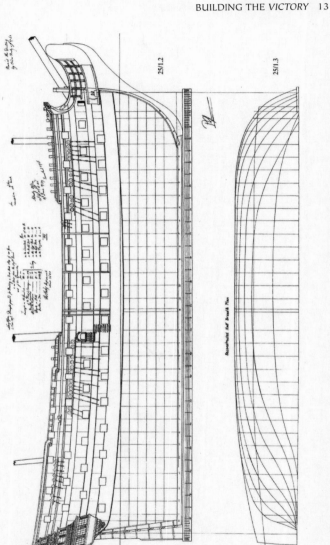

*Sheer draught and half breadth plan of HMS* Victory, *as built in 1765*

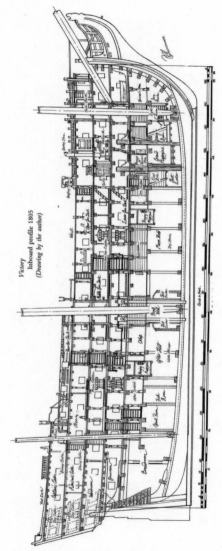

Victory *inboard profile cross-section*

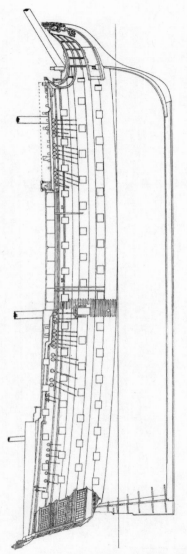

*Victory lines profile, 1803–1805*

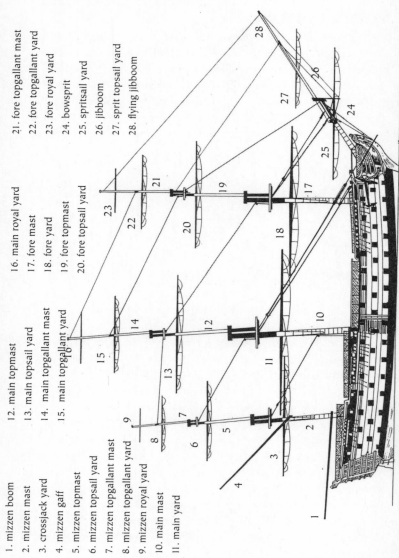

1. mizzen boom
2. mizzen mast
3. crossjack yard
4. mizzen gaff
5. mizzen topmast
6. mizzen topsail yard
7. mizzen topgallant mast
8. mizzen topgallant yard
9. mizzen royal yard
10. main mast
11. main yard

12. main topmast
13. main topsail yard
14. main topgallant mast
15. main topgallant yard
16. main royal yard
17. fore mast
18. fore yard
19. fore topmast
20. fore topsail yard

21. fore topgallant mast
22. fore topgallant yard
23. fore royal yard
24. bowsprit
25. spritsail yard
26. jibboom
27. sprit topsail yard
28. flying jibboom

*Victory masts and yards*

## TIMBER AND MATERIALS

Some 300,000 cubic feet of timber were used in the construction of the hull of a first-rate ship like the *Victory* before its conversion into the many separate components. This equates to 6000 trees taken from 100 acres of woodland, 90 per cent of which was English oak. The best oak came from the Weald forests of Kent and Sussex. This could easily shipped on barges down the River Medway to the dockyard at Chatham. Kent and Sussex oak was particularly good as the native heavy weald clay soil promoted slow growth to produce a dense robust timber.

*How timber component sections were cut from trees.*

As well as English elm, which was used for the keel, other timbers included pine, fir and spruce, most of which were imported from the Baltic States together with straight oak from Danzig (modern Gdansk). Beech was also used, although it was not ideal. Pine for the *Victory's* great lower masts would at this particular period still have been imported from New England, where single trees, growing some 130 feet in height and three feet in diameter could be readily sourced to form 'pole' masts. After the American Declaration of Independence in 1776 this source of mast timber was restricted for the duration of the resultant war.

Other materials needed in great quantities for the ship's hull were iron nails, spikes and bolts; also copper bolts of up to two inches in diameter, some being 10 feet long. Vast quantities of iron or copper roves (washers) were needed for use with the bolts, the iron coming from England's extensive resources. While some copper may have originated from Sweden, most was now sourced from the expanding Welsh copper industry.

## THE *VICTORY* IS LAUNCHED

The *Victory's* hull was completed on St George's Day, 23 April 1765. On 28 April Master Shipwright Edward Allin wrote to the Navy Board stating: *'His Majesty's Ship Victory building in the Old single Dock will be ready to launch the ensuing Spring tydes.'* Invitations for the launch were sent to the prime minister William Pitt the Elder, members of his cabinet and members of both houses in Parliament, all of whom travelled by coach to Chatham for the ceremony. The *Victory* was duly 'launched' on Tuesday 7 May 1765. News of the launch was published in the *London Public Advertiser*:

*'This day will be launched his majesties ship the* Victory, *estimated the largest and finest ship ever built. Several of the Lords of the Admiralty, Commissioners of the Navy, and many persons of quality and distinction, are expected to be present, for whose receptions great preparations are making through the Town.'*

*Victory* was not actually launched in the broadest sense, but simply 'floated off' the dock. At this period, all first-rate ships were actually built within an enclosed dry dock as they were too large to construct in the conventional manner on a slipway. The overall cost of the *Victory* including masts, yards, rigging and stores etc. amounted to £63,176. 3s.0d. Today, this figure would be approximately £46.5 million.

In the same year, the British under Greville introduced the Stamp Act. The Act imposed a direct tax on the British American colonies that required many printed materials in the colonies to use stamped paper produced in London, carrying an embossed revenue stamp, amounting to a tax on all papers required for official transactions.

After initial sea trials the *Victory* was immediately laid up in 'ordinary' (reserve) and spent the next 13 years moored in the River Medway during which time she suffered problems with rotting planking.

# 2

# *VICTORY'S* SEA SERVICE:

## THE REVOLUTIONARY WAR OF AMERICAN INDEPENDENCE, 1778

The *Victory* first saw action during this war at the First Battle of Ushant when France entered the conflict in support of the American rebel colonists.

While *'Lying at Moorings at Gillingham'* on the River Medway below Chatham, *Victory* received her first commander Captain John Lindsay who entered the ship on 12 March 1778: *'At 1 PM Came down here, hoisted the Pendant on Board His Majestys Ship Victory & put her in Commission'.* The ship was then fully prepared for sea service as the flagship of Admiral Augustus Keppel. On 27 April 1778 Lindsay recorded: *'at 8 Came on Board His Majesty'* (George III) *attended by Lord Sandwich'* (John Montagu the fourth Earl Sandwich and First Lord of the Admiralty) who inspected the ship and officers. After 11 days taking on all manner of stores water and gunpowder at Blackstakes anchorage at the mouth of the Medway the *Victory 'weighed & made Sail'*, on 8 May, for Portsmouth and made her way along the north coast of Kent, passing the North Foreland on Saturday 9 May. With weather moderate and cloudy, on Sunday 10 May, the *Victory* suffered her first casualty: *'Employed Tiding down Channel ½ past 3 John Smith fell over Board & was drowned.'*

### First Battle of Ushant: Monday 27 July 1778

When Admiral Augustus Keppel hoisted his flag in the *Victory* at Portsmouth, command of the ship was given over to Captain Jonathan Faulkner. Appointed as flagship of the Channel Fleet the *Victory* sailed from Spithead on 9 July 1778 with 29 ships of the line. Second in command was Admiral Sir Hugh Palliser flying his flag in the *Formidable* (90 guns). On 23 July Keppel sighted a French fleet of similar force 100 miles (160 km) west of Ushant under Admiral Louis Guillouet, Comte d'Orvilliers flying his flag in *Le Bretagne* (110 guns).

Although d'Orvilliers had the 'weather gauge' (wind advantage) he was cut off from getting into Brest. Hampered by shifting winds, heavy rain squalls and poor visibility, the two fleets finally manoeuvred to engage in battle, the British sailing in column, with the French passing along the British line to windward. Before battle commenced, Faulkner '*Served an Allowance of Grog to the Ship's Company*' and *at '½ past 11 got alongside the Bretagne and at Noon engaging the Ville de Paris*' (90 guns). After the *Victory* had delivered thunderous broadsides into these two great ships she moved on to engage six ships astern of d'Orvilliers' flagship. The *Victory* had received her 'baptism of fire'.

As a result of poor visibility and contrary winds both fleets were unable to fully engage in close action. Keppel then signalled the fleet to wear (turn) and follow the French, but Admiral Sir Hugh Palliser, leading the rear division, failed to comply, with the result that close action was not wholly sustained and although the British vanguard had escaped with little loss, Admiral Palliser's division unfortunately suffered considerably as a consequence. As this first major naval engagement with France within this war proved indecisive the outcome led to political repercussions in both countries. Palliser, criticised by an inquiry, turned the affair into a Whig-Tory argument, while Keppel was court-martialled and cleared.

## Second Battle of Ushant: Wednesday 12 December 1781

In 1781 the *Victory* served as flagship to Rear Admiral Richard Kempenfelt. Operating with a squadron of 12 ships of the line, Kempenfelt intercepted a French convoy of transports and troopships bound from Brest for the East and West Indies. These were escorted by 19 warships, commanded by Admiral Luc Urbain de Bouëxic, Comte de Guichen.

'*Fresh Gales and thick hazey [sic] We Exchang'd Broadsides with one of the Enemy's line of Battle Ships as [they] passed us to leeward and brought to [stopped] several of the Convoy.*' Although Kempenfelt's squadron was numerically inferior his ships successfully managed to capture 15 transports, 1063 soldiers and 548 seamen from under the noses of the escorting squadron.

## Battle of Cape Spartel: Sunday 20 October 1782

In *Victory's* final engagement during the American War of Independence she was serving as flagship to Admiral Richard Howe. Although Gibraltar had been under constant siege since 1779, it had been consistently supplied by ships and transports of the Royal Navy. During the third relief operation Howe's fleet of 35 ships of the line met with the combined fleets of France and Spain, comprising 38 line of battle ships commanded by Admiral Luis de Córdova y Córdova. Although the ensuing battle proved indecisive, Gibraltar was successfully resupplied.

# THE FRENCH REVOLUTIONARY WAR

Commencing in 1793 the *Victory* spent the earlier part of this war as flagship to Admirals Hyde Parker, Alexander Hood, John Mann, Robert Linzee and Sir John Jervis. Until 1797 *Victory* was mainly deployed in the Mediterranean, involved with both the siege and later the blockade of Toulon, the Corsican Campaign and the Battle of Hyères.

## Battle of Hyères: Monday 13 July 1795

This took place off the Hyères islands in the Mediterranean about 16 miles (25km) east of Toulon. This battle involved a combined British Neapolitan squadron of 17 line of battle ships and six frigates commanded by Vice-Admiral Hotham, flying his flag in the 100-gun *Britannia* and a French squadron of 23 sail of the line and 15 frigates under the command of Rear-Admiral Pierre Martin. Second in command of the British was Rear-Admiral Robert Mann in the *Victory*, under the command of Captain John Knight.

On sighting the French, Hotham immediately signalled to give chase and a running battle followed. Knight recorded: 'AM *1-10 recommenced firing on the Sternmost Ships, the Culloden began to fire, employed engaging the Enemy ... at 12 the sternmost Ship of the Enemy we were engaging struck her colours and ceased firing.'* This was the French ship, the *Alcide* (74-guns).

Knight's log then states: '*a frigate attempted to take her in tow fired on the frigate ¼ pt. 2 observed the Prize on fire in the Fore Top.*'

The *Alcide* then exploded, killing some 300 men. Despite having the advantage, Hotham called off the action. British casualties were light, with 11 killed and 28 wounded. Next day, two of the fleeing French ships collided, one being the 84-gun *Ça Ira*. Nelson, present during the battle in command of the 64-gun *Agamemnon*, took the opportunity to engage the *Ça Ira* for two and a half hours before two French ships arrived, forcing him to veer away.

## Battle of Cape St Vincent: Tuesday 14 February 1797

Although part of the French Revolutionary War, this battle relates to the Anglo-Spanish War of 1796–1808. The Spanish declaration of war on Britain and Portugal in October 1796 made the British position in the Mediterranean untenable. In this battle the *Victory* was serving as flagship to Admiral Sir John Jervis commanding a British squadron of 15 ships of the line, five frigates, a sloop and an armed cutter that fought against a Spanish fleet of 24 ships of the line, seven frigates, one brig and four armed merchantmen under the command of Admiral Don José de Córdoba y Ramos.

This action took place off Cape St Vincent, Portugal. Seeing his fleet around him formed into two lines of battle on the morning of the battle, Jervis turned to his officers on the quarter-deck of the *Victory* and said, *'A victory to England is very essential at this moment'* He then ordered the fleet to prepare for action. At 11.00am, Jervis signalled: *'Form in a line of battle ahead and astern of* Victory *as most convenient.'* The British fleet formed a single line of battle, sailing in a southerly course to pass between the two Spanish columns. At 11.12am, Jervis made his next signal: *'Engage the enemy.'* Then, at 11.30am, he signalled: *'The Admiral intends to pass through enemy lines.'* Unprepared and formed into two groups, the Spanish were tactically disadvantaged by this manoeuvre as the British ships could fire into them in both directions. At 12.08pm Jervis ordered the fleet to tack in succession to bear down upon the leeward side of the Spanish ships. *Victory's* log states: *'At 12.15pm the action became general from van to centre.'* Throughout the battle *Victory* added her weight of broadsides as opportunity arose, her main contender being the *Salvador Del Mundo*.

During this contest the 112-gun *Principe de Asturias* closed to engage the *Victory*. However, her admiral lost his nerve and, in turning away, exposed his ship to a thunderous broadside from the *Victory*. The great Spanish ship was reduced to a shambles and with her steering shot away and rudder jammed she turned yet again to receive a second devastating delivery from the *Victory* and fell away to leeward totally out of action. Recording this event, *Victory's* log states: *'Raked her both ahead and astern he appeared in great confusion and bore up, as did the other Spanish ships.'* At one point in the battle the Spanish were in a position to escape but Nelson, then commanding the 74-gun *Captain*, saw this potential flaw and turned his ship out of the line of battle in an attempt to cut off their retreat. Nelson then put his ship across the path of the mighty four-decker 136-gun *Nuestra Senora de Santísima Trinidad*, forcing the Spanish ships to alter course, the 80-gun *San Nicolas* and 112-gun *San Josef* colliding. Nelson immediately put his much-damaged *Captain* alongside the *San Nicolas* and, leading his men, boarded her, forcing her to capitulate. After taking possession of the *San Nicolas* he then crossed the deck and boarded the *San Josef*.

Nelson's initiative in preventing the Spanish escaping brought about a victory for Jervis. Had the attempt failed he would have faced a court-martial for disobeying orders to stay in the rigid line of battle. Casualties on the British side amounted to 73 dead and 327 wounded; the Spanish suffered four ships captured, 250 dead, 550 wounded and 3000 taken prisoner. The *Victory's* final battle in the Napoleonic War at Trafalgar in 1805 is covered in Chapter 15.

## THE RUSSO-SWEDISH WAR OF 1808-09

### The Baltic Campaign and Peninsular War

Much damaged at Trafalgar, the *Victory* was towed to Gibraltar by the 98-gun *Neptune* and finally returned to Portsmouth on 4 December, bearing her fallen hero. After repairs at Chatham costing £9936, the *Victory* was re-commissioned in March 1808. Reclassified as a second-rate ship of 98 guns *Victory* completed her 'Account of Iron Ordnance' on Saturday 5 March 1808, her guns being embarked over the previous days. While many of the guns were either new or reconditioned, a few of those returned had been on the ship at Trafalgar (only seven remain today). Not only was her armament reduced: all her middle gun deck armament 24-pounders were replaced with lighter 18-pounders. This was done for four reasons:

1. To deploy her 24s into other ships on active service.

2. To reduce the weight of ordnance carried within an aging hull which itself reflected on both powder, and shot borne.

3. Eighteen-pounders required a smaller guns crew, thereby reducing both crew and provisions carried.

4. Fewer crew provided more room for carrying troops.

Now the flagship of Admiral Sir James Saumarez, this commission saw *Victory* undertaking operations in the Baltic supporting Sweden against the Russians. In September 1808 the *Victory* was deployed in the Baltic with the

*Goliath* (74 guns), Mars (74 guns) *Africa* (64 guns) and flotilla of Swedish warships standing off the port of Ragervik (modern-day Paldiski in Estonia) into which Admiral Chanykov's Russian squadron had taken refuge. Saumarez attempted to attack using bomb vessels firing mortar shells into the town and ships, but as little harm was done the allies resorted to maintaining a blockade.

Following the retreat of Sir John Moore's army from French forces in Spain at the beginning of the Peninsular War the *Victory* was sent out with transports to Vigo evacuate the remnants of Moore's army from Corunna, returning home on 23 January 1809. In April she was back in the Baltic for the blockade of the Russian fleet in Kronstadt.

## ANGLO-SWEDISH WAR (1810–1812)

When the Swedish Crown Prince Charles August died in May 1810, he was succeeded by Emperor Napoleon Bonaparte's cousin and former Marshall Jean-Baptiste Bernadotte, who was elected Crown Prince of Sweden. Sweden, politically allied to Britain, now automatically became allied to France and declared war on Britain in November 1810. This forced Britain to continue deploying the *Victory* and other ships in the Baltic blockading the Swedish navy in Karlscrona. However, as Sweden's relationship with France was deteriorating under Bernadotte's rule, retaining Saumarez on this station proved a diplomatic advantage. In 1811, *Victory* was temporarily withdrawn and converted into a troopship transporting reinforcements to Lisbon for Wellington's army in the Peninsula War. When France occupied Swedish Pomerania and the island of Rügen in 1812, Bernadotte, aided by Saumarez, sought peace with Britain. No longer needed and now 47 years old, *Victory* was recalled, finally returning to Portsmouth on Friday 4 December 1812 and '*payed off* 16 days later and laid up in ordinary to await her fate.

## POST SEA SERVICE

Between 1814 and 1816, *Victory* was rebuilt with much alteration. The ornate beakhead bulkhead was replaced with a more practical round bow, her bulwarks were built up square and her sides were painted with black and white horizontal stripes. The war with France finally at an end, she was placed back into 'ordinary' (laid up in reserve) until 1824. The *Victory* then took on a new role as flagship for the Port Admiral and later tender to the *Duke of Wellington*. In 1831 the ship was listed for disposal, but Hardy, now First Sea Lord, at his wife's request refused to sign and gave the *Victory* her second reprieve. Refitted in 1888, she was recoppered for the fifteenth and last time. The following year she became flagship for the Commander in Chief. Today she is flagship for the First Sea Lord.

Disaster struck in 1903 when she was accidentally rammed by the iron warship *Neptune* which was under tow to the breakers. After e,mergency docking she went back to her familiar moorings. This event, together with the ensuing centenary of Trafalgar, raised questions about her future; however, the First World War intervened. Finally, through a national appeal raised by the Society for Nautical Research, the *Victory* was put into her current dock on Thursday 12 January 1922 and restored to her 1805 appearance as a living monument to the Royal Navy. After completing her second phase of restoration, the *Victory* was suitably equipped throughout with a vast range of artifacts, weapons, tools and domestic necessities that provide an accurate interpretation of life at sea within Nelson's ships for the bicentenary of Trafalgar in 2005.

## REFIT HISTORY

In March 1780 the *Victory*'s hull was sheathed with 3923 sheets of copper below the waterline to protect it against shipworm, adding some 17 tons to her weight. Although this measure also improved speed by deterring the build-up crustaceans it did initially cause new problems with iron hull fittings, *Victory* being no exception. A letter dated 1 March 1783 discussed this:

*'But on the* Victory *being lately carried into Dock, it is found, That all the Bolts for 4 to 5 Inches inwards from the Copper, is sound and all the rest inwards to the Hold, nothing but rust and it is the general opinion of the Officers and Carpenters, who have inspected her, that had she touched the Ground ever so slightly she must have gone to pieces.'*

In March 1783, the *Victory* was recalled and went into refit at a cost of £15,372 19s. 9d. During this time her quarterdeck armament of six-pounder guns was changed to short 12-pounders. Her sides, originally painted 'bright' with rosin down to the top of the lower-deck gun ports, were now painted a dull yellow ochre including the external faces of her gun port lids; the ship's side below this point was painted black. Although the *Victory* had been coppered, it had been found that many of the copper-sheathed ships were suffering with corroded iron hull fastenings caused by the electrolytic reaction between the copper and iron hull fittings. Subsequently *Victory's* iron fittings were replaced during this refit with those of copper at an estimated cost of £2500.

In 1787 the ship underwent a 'large repair' at a cost of £37,523 17s. 1d. During this refit the ship was further strengthened by fitting breadth, middle and top riders which provided additional internal bracing to her hull between the orlop deck and the upper gun deck to counteract the inherent hogging and sagging effects on an aging hull that was now 22 years old. Evidence shows that these additional riders were still present in the ship at Trafalgar but later removed. Her foremast was also moved further aft to rebalance her rigging in relation to the newly introduced flying jibboom; this necessitated lengthening her forecastle aft. Recommissioned in 1789, the ship again served as flagship to Admiral Howe and flagship to Admiral Hood in 1790.

# 3

# ENTERING THE SHIP AND THE GEORGIAN NAVY

## THE OFFICERS

The majority of naval officers came from the English sea counties of Devon, Hampshire and Kent with their naval dockyards at Plymouth, Portsmouth, and Chatham. These counties also contained the seats of influential families; consequently the overall background of those who served as naval officers came from two distinctive social groups:

1. peers, baronets and landed gentry;
2. professional men, commercial businessmen and the clergy.

Examples of the latter group include Admirals Jervis, Nelson, Collingwood, Pellew and Strachan, likewise Captains Ball, Blackwood and Hoste.

Potential officers entered the service by one of two methods; indirectly through the Royal Naval College at Portsmouth, which opened in 1729, or directly through voluntary enlistment into ships as 'servants'. Despite the existence of the naval academy, the long-tested system whereby volunteers were enlisted directly into a ship as 'captain's servants' or First Class Volunteers remained standard practice until 1794, Nelson being one of these.

## THE SEAMEN

The popular conception that most of the seamen serving on the *Victory's* 'lower deck' were conscripts forced into the 'Kings Navy' by bullying press gangs is frequently misleading. Most men entering the Royal Navy, either by impressment or simply as volunteers, were professional seamen and men coming from sea-related trades. Many would have served within the mercantile and fishing fleets or came from areas with some connection to the naval dockyards. Unlike the officers, who had influence and advantage, the common seamen simply needed full-time paid employment and although pay in the Merchant service was higher, the Royal Navy did have reasonable advantages. As well as the catchment counties of Cornwall, Devon, Hampshire and Kent, a large number of seamen came from the dockside areas of London, such as Wapping.

The majority of the *Victory's* ship's company of 820 officers (the Admiral excluded), marines, seamen and landsmen originated from the British Isles. Besides the English, there were men of Scots, Irish, Welsh and Manx origin. In all, this totalled 700 men or 85 per cent of the entire ship's company crew.

| *Origins of* **Victory's ship's company within the British Isles** | | |
|---|---|---|
| *Origin* | *Number* | *Percentage of crew total of 820* |
| *English* | *514* | *62.68* |
| *Irish* | *88* | *10.73* |
| *Manx* | *1* | *0.12* |
| *Scots* | *67* | *8.20* |
| *Welsh* | *30* | *3.65* |
| *TOTAL* | *700* | *85.36* |

Added to these were men of various nationalities from merchant ships who, perhaps left in a foreign port without a ship, were pressed into service by captains desperately short of crew. Many were of Northern European or Scandinavian origin, together with Italians or Maltese with reason to oppose France. The table on the right provides a good insight into the various countries of origin forming the *Victory's* ship's company.

| International origins of Victory's ship's company | | |
|---|---|---|
| Nationality | Number | Percentage |
| African | 1 | 0.12 |
| American | 22 | 2.75 |
| Brazilian | 1 | 0.12 |
| Canadian | 2 | 0.24 |
| Danish | 2 | 0.24 |
| Dutch | 7 | 0.85 |
| English | 514 | 62.68 |
| French | 4 | 0.49 |
| German | 2 | 0.24 |
| Indian | 2 | 0.24 |
| Irish | 88 | 10.73 |
| Italian | 9 | 1.10 |
| Jamaican | 1 | 0.12 |
| Maltese | 6 | 0.73 |
| Manx | 1 | 0.12 |
| Norwegian | 2 | 0.24 |
| Portuguese | 1 | 0.12 |
| Scots | 67 | 8.20 |
| Swedish | 4 | 0.49 |
| Swiss | 2 | 0.24 |
| West Indian | 4 | 0.49 |
| Welsh | 30 | 3.65 |
| Unrecorded | 48 | 5.85 |
| TOTAL | 820 | |

Note: Ironically, four of the Victory's crew were actually Frenchmen, these being Royalist émigrés.

## VOLUNTEERS

Consisting of both men and boys, this group generally joined for patriotic reasons, or was attracted by the promise of adventure and travel together with the prospect of a steady wage. Volunteers, as shown in many of the contemporary recruiting posters, were enticed by receiving a bounty of up to £20, an upfront payment equivalent to one year's wages for a labourer. Other volunteers, perhaps less nobly, did so to escape the law; lured by the bounty to pay their debts, they could avoid prison. Despite the hardships that would follow, the reputation of a bold ship's captain also encouraged volunteers, especially if he was known to capture prize ships where all crew received a proportional share additional to their earnings.

The boy volunteers (not to be confused with those who joined with the intention of becoming an officer) had mostly been turned out of their homes or run away and, with few prospects other than crime, the navy was a better alternative. Many of these boys entered into the navy from the Marine Society set up by Jonas Hanway in 1756 which provided an orphanage for waifs and strays. At the age of 12 these lads were provided with a bible and nautical clothing and sent into the navy as Third Class volunteer boys, initially becoming officer's servants earning about £4 per year. Conditioned to life at sea from an early age these boys naturally became first-rate Royal Navy seamen.

## THE IMPRESSMENT SERVICE

Conscription into the Georgian navy came in two forms: impressment or the Quota Acts. The Impressment Service, supported by its main instrument the 'press gang', was often portrayed a despicable organisation with a popular consensus generated by misguided historians or somewhat over-dramatised in contemporary caricatures, film and television.

In truth, impressment was the fundamental organisation that provided the government with the power to call upon its subjects to defend the sovereign state during times of war; these days, it is often termed conscription.

### The press gang ashore

The word 'press' is often misused. It originates from the French verb *prêter*, to lend or give money in return for service, similar to receiving the King's shilling 'prest' into the hand when enlisting into the army. Because the long war with

France had greatly increased demand for manpower, press gangs became far more active, some using force to assemble sufficient numbers of men. What the press gangs were after were good seamen who knew ships and how to live in them: tough men who knew how to knot and splice rope and hand sails; men from the mercantile and fishing fleet were a prime target. On shore, the press gang operated from a 'rendezvous' commanded by a lieutenant from the ship with a group of loyal seamen: the Wrestlers' Arms in Great Yarmouth was a popular example and the place from where James Sharman, later to serve as an ordinary seaman in the *Victory* at Trafalgar, was recruited. Sharman, together with James Secker, a Royal Marine Sergeant, carried Lord Nelson down to the ship's cockpit after the admiral was fatally shot.

So needy was the navy for people at this period that it was not unusual to find the impressment service setting up 'recruiting stations' in towns further inland. Groups of pressed men were often first sent into a 'receiving ship' where they were 'regulated' before being entered into a commissioned ship. The regulating process evaluated the potential status: able or ordinary seaman according to ability or experience, inexperienced men being rated as 'landsmen'. A man would be enrolled to receive pay but given the opportunity to sign on as a 'volunteer'. He would also receive the promised bounty in addition; most took this option. If a man was married, arrangements were made to ensure his wife received a regular allotment of money; otherwise they would have had to rely on the parish or poor relief in the man's absence or, worse, turn to prostitution.

The regulating process not only provided suitable clothing, it also determined the physical condition of the men for, despite the urgent need for recruits, the navy did not want weaklings. It was not unusual for 25 per cent of the men 'pressed in' to be immediately discharged as unfit for service. Some were perhaps already suffering from scurvy, which was often thought of as a seaman's disease, but was equally rife on land, especially during the winter season when many people's diet was quite poor.

Certain tradesmen including shipwrights and apprentices, held protection papers that absolved them from service. Although this would guarantee their liberty this was not always the case. Shipwrights bringing a new-built vessel into Portsmouth dockyard from a private Hampshire shipbuilder's yard were seized by the press and incarcerated in a receiving hulk. A petition supported by strike action eventually brought about their release.

Captains desperately short of crew numbers when imminently ready to sail might initiate what was colloquially termed a 'hot press'. This comprised a lieutenant commanding a group of petty officers, seamen and marines who were sent on shore by boat to search taverns and other haunts for unfortunate victims. As they were often compelled to use more force than necessary, it was these 'hot press' gangs that gave the press its historic notoriety.

## The press gang afloat

If insufficient men could be found on land the alternative was to conscript men by impressment afloat; the sea always proved more productive. In the English Channel it was not unusual for captains of undermanned men-of-war to target homebound merchant vessels for manpower. Having been ordered to '*heave-to in the King's name*', naval boarding parties would press the best seamen out of the unfortunate vessel, sometimes leaving few crewmen to handle the ship. Compared with land-based impressment, the press gang afloat could always secure prime seamen. Such practices were later portrayed fictitiously in the play and film *Billy Budd*.

## The quota men

As the war progressed it became necessary to supplement the efforts of the Impressment Service by introducing the Quota Acts. Passed by William Pitt the Younger in 1795, this statute authorised each county, city and specific large towns to provide a predetermined quota of men into the navy per annum according to demand. London, for example, had to enlist some 5,700 men whereas less populated areas such as Yorkshire, had only to provide a fifth of this figure. Although conscription was aimed at recruiting seafarers, bounties had to be offered to entice other volunteers. These, which stood at around £5 in 1793, rose to as much as £70 by the end of the eighteenth century.

# 4

# MANNING THE SHIP

## THE COMMISSIONED OFFICERS

*'Every officer from the time of joining the Ship to which he shall be appointed, to that of his being discharged from it, is to be constant in his attendance on board, never going out of the ship (except on Public Service) without having obtained permission from the Commanding Officer on board: nor shall he remain out of the Ship during the Night , nor after the setting of the Watch , without having express Permission to do so; nor be absent from the Ship for more than Twenty- four Hours at a time, without the Permission of the Commander in Chief, or the Senior Officer present.'*

### The captain

When the *Victory* recommissioned in 1803 her appointed commanding officer was Samuel Sutton who initially sailed the *Victory* into the Mediterranean. Nelson followed in the frigate *Amphion* commanded by his friend, the respected Captain Thomas Masterman Hardy. Finally entering into the *Victory* as his flagship in July 1803, Nelson replaced Sutton with Captain Hardy, sending Sutton into the *Amphion*.

Captain Hardy commanded complete autonomy in the *Victory* on all matters of sailing, operation, organisation and discipline of the crew. The *Admiralty Regulations and Instructions* under which captains worked are far too comprehensive to disclose here. However, each month the captain would inspect and countersign all muster books, pay books and expense books held by the various personnel concerned. Besides overseeing all disciplinary needs and acting as a judicial mediator, he was directly responsible for maintaining the welfare of the ship's company. In accord with the *Articles of War,* he was duty bound to hold Divine Service every Sunday for the entire ship's company. After this service the captain was likewise duty bound to read the entire *Articles of War* to the ship's company to ensure that good order and discipline fully prevailed.

As Captain Hardy did not keep watches at sea, but could be called on deck as required by his subordinate officers on whatever the situation or occasion dictated. In battle Hardy took station on the quarterdeck where his authority was paramount despite the ferocity of the action. Directly under Hardy were nine lieutenants.

## The first lieutenant

This was John Pasco, born in December 1774, who entered the navy on 4 June 1784 as captain's servant in the 32-gun frigate, HMS *Druid*. After serving in various ships, by 1790 he had risen to the rank of midshipman in HMS *Syren* and served in various ships as master's mate and midshipman. Promoted to lieutenant on 15 July 1795 he was assigned into the 74-gun ship HMS *Majestic*. He was entered into the *Victory* on 7 April 1803. Although first lieutenant at Trafalgar, he was assigned as signal officer to provide opportunity to Lieutenant Quilliam. Recording the battle's events Pasco wrote:

'*His Lordship came to me on the poop, and after ordering certain signals to be made, about quarter to noon, he said "Mr Pasco I wish to say to the fleet, ENGLAND CONFIDES THAT EVERY MAN WILL DO HIS DUTY" and he added, "You must be quick, for I have one more to make which is for close action." I replied "If your Lordship will permit me to substitute the word confides for EXPECTS the signal will soon be completed because the word expects is in the [signal] vocabulary and confides must be spelt out" . 'His lordship replied, "that will do make it directly".' This later became the famous 'England expects' signal.*

Despite being wounded in his right side and arm with grapeshot and carried belowdecks at Trafalgar, Pasco later commanded HMS *Mediator* and *Hindustan*. Rising through the ranks he was placed in command of the *Victory* at Portsmouth in 1846 and promoted to Rear Admiral of the Blue the next year.

As first lieutenant Pasco was directly accountable to the captain for the *Victory's* administration of the crew and maintaining a daily ship's routine, allocating where the men were berthed, ensuring the ship's cleanliness and maintaining discipline. He also set out the watch and quarter bills, listing where all officers, seamen and marines were stationed when on watch or in battle. The first lieutenant did not generally keep watches but was obliged to be on deck for any reason determined by the officer of the watch. In battle, the first lieutenant normally stood on the quarter deck with the captain. Should the captain fall, the first lieutenant instantly assumed command of the ship.

## The other lieutenants

The remaining lieutenants undertook watch-keeping duties on deck related to the ship's operation, general navigation and sail handling. In battle, each took command of one gun deck, responsible for the firing control of all guns. Aided by midshipmen and quarter gunners, they ensured that all guns had their equipment and that a constant supply of powder and shot was maintained. Of equal importance, they ensured that the men manning the guns remained steady while under fire from the enemy. Lieutenants not appointed to specific gun decks either took command of the guns on the forecastle or quarter deck while another, appointed as the communications officer, was stationed on the poop deck overseeing the hoists of signal flags. Each lieutenant had charge over one of the ship's divisions of men and, with the assistance of midshipmen, was responsible for the general welfare of the seamen within his division. *Victory's* lieutenants at Trafalgar are listed below:

| Surname | First name | Age | Origin |
|---------|-----------|-----|--------|
| Bligh | George | 21 | English |
| Browne | George | 21 | English |
| Hills | Alexander | 25 | English |
| King | Andrew | 29 | English |
| Quilliam | John | 34 | Manx |
| Ram | William | 21 | Irish |
| Williams | Edward | 27? | Irish |
| Yule | John | 32 | English |

## The midshipmen

Known as 'the young gentlemen', midshipmen went to sea to become naval officers. Although some came from aristocratic families, most came from the middle classes. Many, like Nelson, who was the son of a clergyman, entered into the navy at the age of 12 or 13. There were 21 midshipmen aged between 16 and 29 serving in the *Victory* at Trafalgar:

| Surname | First name | Age | Origin | Notes |
|---------|-----------|-----|--------|-------|
| Barton | Robert | 20 | Welsh | |
| Bulkeley | Richard | 18 | American | |
| Carslake | William | 20 | English | |
| Cary | Henry | 20 | Irish | |
| Felton | John | 21 | English | |
| Grindall | Festing | 18 | English | |
| Harington | Daniel | 29 | Irish | |
| Lyons | John | 22 | English | |
| Ogilvie | David | 23 | English | |
| Palmer | Alexander | 21 | English | Killed at Trafalgar |
| Picken | Oliver | 21 | English | |
| Poad | James | 16 | English | |
| Pollard | John | 18 | English | |
| Rivers | William | 17 | English | Wounded at Trafalgar |
| Roberts | Richard | 20 | English | |
| Robertson | James | 22 | Scots | |
| Sibbald | James | 19 | Scots | |
| Smith | Robert | 20 | English | Killed at Trafalgar |
| Thovez | Philip | 20 | Italian | |
| Thresher | Thomas | 21 | English | |
| Westphal | George | 20 | English | |
| Note: William Rivers was the son of the ship's gunner, also called William Rivers | | | | |

Besides assisting the officer of the watch, their duties comprised taking charge of the log line, operating the ship's boats and commanding groups of guns. Like the lieutenants, each midshipman was responsible for the welfare and discipline of divisions of seamen.

All midshipmen berthed on the orlop, sleeping in hammocks or cots slung from the beams. Midshipmen aged 14 or over, called 'oldsters', messed together at tables set up in the after cockpit. Mealtimes in this mess were often boisterous occasions. Midshipmen of lesser age, nicknamed 'youngsters', generally messed in the gun room at the after end of the lower gun deck under the watchful eye of the gunner.

Midshipman William Rivers was the son of the *Victory's* gunner, William Rivers. During the battle of Trafalgar, Rivers junior's foot was almost completely blown off by a grenade, left attached to him '*by a Piece of Skin abought* [sic] *4 inch above the ankle*'. Rivers asked first for his shoes, then told the gunner's mate to look after the guns and informed Captain Hardy that he was going down to the cockpit. The leg was then amputated without anaesthetic, four inches below the knee, legend stating that he did not cry out once during the operation. Anxious about his son's welfare, gunner Rivers went to the cockpit to ask after him; the young man called out from the other side of the deck, '*Here I am, Father, nothing is the matter with me; only lost my leg and that in a good cause.*'

## NON-COMMISSIONED STANDING OFFICERS
### The master
This was Thomas Atkinson who, '*when appointed to one of His Majesty's Ships, is to be constantly attentive in his duty, and diligently and punctually to execute all orders he may receive from the Captain or any of the Lieutenants of the said Ship, or from any Flag Officer, or the Captain of any other Ship, for his Majesty's service.*' Atkinson had seven master's mates working under him.

### The boatswain
At Trafalgar this man, William Wilmett, was one of the two most senior petty officers on the ship. Wilmett was responsible to the ship's master and captain for all aspects of rigging, sails, blocks, general cordage, anchors and cables, ship's boats and all other matters of seamanship. Besides being highly skilled and experienced in his trade, he was also ranked as one of the ship's standing officers and remained with the ship working as a ship-keeper while the vessel was laid up in ordinary. The practice of retaining certain 'ship-

keepers' maintained continuity and understanding of a particular ship's rigging equipment, information that was invaluable to a new commanding officer and master when a ship was recommissioned. Besides undertaking daily inspections of the rigging, the boatswain ensured that the boatswain's mates, his petty officer assistants, turned the watches of seamen out on deck to attend sail-handling duties and other necessary ship operations.

As a standing officer he had his own cabin, near his expansive storeroom. Holding a vast quantity of stores, equipment, and sails under his charge, he presented monthly accounts to the captain of the items expended in the course of his duties. To avoid fraudulent practices his stores were periodically mustered and inspected by boatswains from other ships. He would also be called upon to administer the same service. One of his main concerns was to ensure that all sails were in good repair, aired and well dried before storing, for if left damp, they could catch fire by spontaneous combustion.

Should the ship be docked for refit or careened, the boatswain had to ensure that all his stores were removed from the ship and transferred to a secure 'lay apart' store designated within the dockyard. On completion he likewise had to muster his equipment and re-embark it into the ship. The times taken to effect the movement of stores in or off the ship are documented in original ship's logbooks that are still in existence today.

The boatswain's other duties, as indicated within the captain's orders of the frigate HMS *Amazon* in 1799, were to ensure that when at anchor the external sides of the ship from stem to stern were '*washed, sweeped and cleared of loose yarns, oakum and every kind of dirt from the gunwale down to the water's edge; and upon all occasions to watch that no clothes lines or ropes whatever are hanging or towing over the chains, gunwales or head.*'

Although mature in years and highly experienced in the execution of their duties it appears that boatswains were frequently in trouble, mainly for drunkenness. In 1808 their annual pay amounted to about £57 12s 0d if serving in a first-rate ship, or £36 12s. 0d. in a sixth-rate ship.

## The gunner

Equal in seniority to the boatswain and often referred to as the master gunner, the man holding this post in the *Victory* in 1805 was William Rivers. As a key man in a first-rate ship of war, his overall responsibilities were extensive as he was fully accountable to the ship's captain for all the ship's ordnance, the magazines, gunpowder, shot, cartridges, gunlocks and other gunnery associated equipment, rockets, and ship's small arms and hand weapons.

Rivers was born in 1755 in the parish of St Mary's Bermondsey in the London borough of Southwark. After serving as a gun captain in various smaller ships Rivers commenced serving in the *Victory* when Britain went to war with revolutionary France in 1793. Like the boatswain, the gunner was a 'standing officer' remaining with the ship when it was laid up in ordinary. This fact is verified by the length of service given by Rivers in the *Victory* between 1793 and 1811 during which time the ship was put in ordinary from 1797 till 1800, rebuilt between 1801 and 1803, and further laid up for repairs between 1806 and 1808. Remaining in the ship until 1811, he was her longest serving man.

Although Rivers' expertise was self-taught, examination of his personal papers shows that he had an intricate knowledge of mathematics and trigonometry related to gunnery ranges and trajectory, and a fine grasp of ballistics and chemistry, along with good practical experience about explosives and projectiles. These papers also indicate that his knowledge was further expanded by receiving periodic training at the Royal Arsenal at Woolwich, where new theories based on recent experimentation and invention were taught. These records also show that Rivers was well trained in chemistry with the ability to create explosive rockets for offensive use and fireworks to make coloured signalling rockets for use at night. Such men as these were the elite in their chosen professional field. Generally 'rough' in nature by virtue of their lower deck background, on the whole gunners were steady, reliable characters much respected by the officers and crew alike. Personal anecdotes and writings show that Rivers was religious and intellectual, a man of his times. He died aged 62, on Wednesday 30 April 1817 in Portsea, Portsmouth.

As a key man in a first-rate ship of war, the articles covering the gunner's overall responsibilities were extensive:

**Article 1** *As soon as one of His Majesty's Ships is ordered to be commissioned, the Gunner is to apply to the Storekeeper of the Ordnance at the Port for the established number of guns, with the proper quantity of ammunition and Stores, which he is to carefully examine before they are put into the hoys* [vessels used to convey stores from shore to ship] *and he is to report to the Storekeeper any imperfection or deficiency he may discover in them.*

**Article 2** Following the above, he attended receiving the guns on board complete with their carriages, '*and placed in its proper Port; No. 1 being the foremost on the larboard side, No. 2 the foremost starboard.*'

**Article 3** Responsible for the state of the magazines he ensured that they were properly fitted and reported any dampness to the commanding officer. Before embarking gunpowder he ensured that no candles were lit throughout the ship and that the galley fires were extinguished. On completion of loading he ensured that respective lightroom doors and scuttles were securely shut, passing all keys to the captain.

**Article 4** Powder was taken on board at the following places: '*Plymouth Sound or Cawsand Bay, Spithead, Blackstakes, Long reach River Thames; and Ships being ordered into Port are to take out there powder before they pass either of those places.*'

**Article 5** When opening magazines the gunner '*is never to go into the Magazine without being ordered to go there. He is never to allow the doors of the Magazine to be opened but by himself; he is not to open them until a proper Officer is in the light-room* [for example the Cook]; *and he is to be very careful in observing that the men going into the Magazine have not about them any thing which can strike fire* [i.e. steel buckled shoes or belts] *and must take care that no Person enters Magazine without wearing leather slippers supplied by the Ordnance.*'

**Article 6** No powder was to be kept in other part of the ship except the magazines '*except that which the Captain shall order to be kept in the powder boxes or powder horns on deck*', i.e. when at battle stations.

**Article 7** The gunner also ensured that when cartridges were being passed up to the guns in their 'cases of wood' that their lids were secure and that magazines' passages were wetted with about two inches of water as a fire precaution.

**Article 8** When at sea the gunner '*is to turn the barrels of powder every three months* [to prevent separation of the nitre from the other ingredients of the powder] *and examine the cartridges*'.

**Article 9** Besides frequently examining the guns, their carriages and their locks (flint firing mechanisms) he also inspected all muskets and other small arms, including cutlasses, 'tomahawks' (axes) and half pikes.

**Article 10** On the matter of ammunition, i.e. solid iron spherical 'round shot', the gunner had to be '*attentive in keeping the shot-racks full of shot; the powder horns and boxes of priming tubs full and that a sufficient quantity of match* [slow match] *primed and ready for being lighted at the shortest notice*'.

**Article 11** When the ship is preparing for battle the gunner '*is to particularly attentive to see that all the quarters are supplied with everything necessary for the service of the gun, the boarders, firemen &c. he is to see that all* [canvas] *screens thoroughly wetted and hung round the hatches* [anti-flash fire precautions], *and from them to the Magazine*[s] *before he opens the Magazine doors.*'

**Article 12** With respect to training the gun's crews, 'exercising the great guns': *he is to see that they perform every part of the exercise with the utmost correctness, particularly explaining to them, and the strongly reinforcing, the necessity of pointing their guns carefully before firing them, and spunging* [sic] *them well, with the touch hole close stopped immediately after they have been fired'.*

Because the gunner held a vast quantity of stores and equipment, he had, like the boatswain, to present monthly accounts to the captain of the items consumed in the course of his duties. He also had to provide accounts covering the quantity of powder, shot or musket ball that was expended for the purpose of gunnery and small arms training. Like the boatswain, the gunner provided monthly store accounts to his captain, was subjected to having his stores periodically inspected by other gunners to check for fraud and gave similar service when called upon to do so.

Should the ship be docked for refit or careened, he had to ensure that all his stores were removed from the ship and temporarily laid apart within the dockyard, likewise all the guns, and afterwards muster his equipment and re-embark it into the ship on completion.

Rivers was also responsible for overseeing the gunner's mates, quarter gunners, yeoman of the powder room, gun captains, and the training of all the gun's crews firing 'at a mark'. Unlike the other two standing officers, the gunner did not have a cabin in the true sense but berthed in an area divided off in the gunroom at the after end of the lower gun deck in two decked ships and above where he messed with the gunner's mates and the junior midshipmen. His annual pay, equal to that of the boatswain, was about £57 12s 0d if serving in a first-rate ship, or £36 12s. 0d. in a sixth-rate ship.

## The purser

*Victory*'s purser, Walter Burke, was born in Limerick and, at the age of 69, was the oldest man serving in the *Victory* at Trafalgar. Burke, who was at Nelson's side when the Admiral was dying, had two sons serving as officers in the Royal

Navy: Henry, who was lost at sea while commanding the sloop HMS *Seagull* in 1805, and Walter, who was killed in action while serving in the 36-gun HMS *Doris* when capturing the French corvette *La Chevrette* in 1801. Burke died 10 years after Trafalgar. He was buried in the churchyard at Wouldham, near Rochester, Kent.

As a senior warrant officer paid at the same rate as a boatswain or gunner, Burke was effectively a civilian provisions manager attached to the ship. He was fully responsible for provisioning the ship with all foodstuffs and drink. This was undertaken at his own personal financial risk as all pursers initially purchased all provisions from the Navy Board victuallers at their own expense before seeking compensation from the Admiralty. Although they also profited by providing the seamen and marines slop clothing, bedding, hammocks, candles and tobacco at cost, many still became bankrupt through the loss or deterioration of provisions.

As a businessman Burke equally ensured that he took his own precautions against financial loss. A commission of 12½ per cent per weight of provisions issued was accepted practice. Some people believed that pursers fraudulently short-measured the crew by issuing 14 rather than the statutory 16 ounces to the pound weight, the difference of one-eighth legitimately accounting for 'ordinary wastage'. Although some pursers obviously used this to their advantage, many went bankrupt in their attempt to keep within the legitimate guidelines. Short measure of victuals was one of the grievances petitioned by the seamen in the Great Mutiny April 1797. As a result, in June, pursers were officially instructed to *'lay aside the ancient weights and measures pursuant to public order'*, which virtually abolished the 14-ounce pound.

Besides issuing hammocks and bedding, for which the seamen paid, the purser also issued slop clothing on which he made a commission of five per cent. He also made money on tobacco of which each man was entitled to two pounds per lunar month; retailing it at 1s. 7d. (8p) per pound, his commission was 10 per cent. In the *Victory* with an estimated tobacco issue of 20,400lb per annum at an estimated retail cost of £1615, 10 per cent of this sum would provide Burke with an estimated profit of £161 10s. Considering Burke's annual income averaged only £47 2s. 0d., receiving the 10 per cent income from the sale of tobacco was quite lucrative.

Burke also held a special allowance to procure coal and wood for the galley fire hearth and heating stoves for officer's cabins and the lower deck, lanthorns, candles and moulds for making them, and 'turnery', which comprised wooden eating implements for the crew, bowls, plates and spoons etc. Assisting the purser was the ship's steward who berthed in the issue room adjacent to the bread room. As he was often covered in flour, he was colloquially called 'Jack o' the Dust', giving rise to the modern naval idiom 'Jack Dusty' for a man rated as store-man.

## The carpenter

This was William Bunce who was born in 1750 at St Mary's, Pembroke, Wales and died on 6 May 1832 at Stoke, Devonport, Plymouth. As the third standing officer, the carpenter differed from the boatswain and gunner as he would have served a seven-year apprenticeship learning his entire profession on shore and therefore originally came from a civilian social background. In most cases, he would have spent at least a further seven years working at his trade of carpenter or shipwright before entering the navy.

To be appointed carpenter on a specific ship he must have least, *'served an apprenticeship to a shipwright, and has been six calendar months a carpenter's mate of one or more of His Majesty's ships'*. Naturally quite a number of these men had actually worked within the Royal or private dockyards, or had been impressed from merchant ships.

Like the boatswain and gunner, the carpenter also had to hold a vast quantity of stores and equipment and presented his monthly accounts of the items consumed in the course of his duties to the ship's captain. His store room was always located near the boatswain's store on the fore platform of the orlop. Besides his specialist range of tools, the carpenter's stores comprised a vast assortment of nails, bolts, copper and lead sheathing, paint, door locks, glass, glue, tar and pitch. He also kept considerable quantities of timber for hull repairs and spare spars, the latter of which was actually pre-prepared timber roughed down to size ready for replacing specific yards or topmasts pertinent to his particular ship's mast specifications.

One of the many tasks the carpenter had to attend to was fitting 'fishes', a form of splint, to masts that had sprung (cracked) during severe wind conditions. As with the other two standing officers, the carpenter's stores were regularly inspected by other carpenters to check for fraud. Unlike the main body of the ship's crew, the carpenter did not keep watches. Being a day worker, he was what was termed an 'idler'.

Besides general repairs his regular daily duty was to sound the water level in the within the ship's well to determine water ingress into the hold and get it pumped overboard. Consequently, he was responsible for the entire maintenance of the pumps, for if they failed the ship's watertight integrity and safety could be disastrously compromised and accumulated filthy bilge water would also have a detrimental effect on the health of the crew. To assist him, he had a carpenter's crew, the number of which varied according to the size of ship.

When the ship went into battle the carpenter and his crew stationed themselves in the lower regions of the ship where, armed with wads of oakum, nails, sheet lead and wooden bungs, they worked plugging shot holes below the waterline. This particular responsibility, first officially authorised during the reign of Queen Elizabeth I, is not dissimilar to that performed by the damage control parties employed on modern warships.

When the ship was docked for refit or careened, the carpenter would ensure that the hull was well supported with timber shores, and if receiving new masts, each mast would be securely stepped and wedged at all deck levels. While he received the same pay as the boatswain and gunner of fourth-rate ships and below, his monthly earnings were £1 more in larger ships, giving him an annual wage of £69 18s. 0d.

# OTHER NON-COMMISSIONED STANDING OFFICERS

## The armourer

The *Victory's* armourer was James Cepell, aged 35 when he entered the ship. His title originated from the person who looked after body armour and weapons.

By the early nineteenth century the armourer was directly responsible to the gunner for the maintenance and repair of all the ship's inventory of hand weapons and small arms, which comprised muskets (with their bayonets), pistols, cutlasses, half pikes and axes (commonly listed as tomahawks). Associated equipment included scabbards, frogs, slings, belts, flints and cartridges for muskets, and pistols. Prior to battle the armourer issued and distributed weapons for boarding parties. He was also responsible for the spring-operated mechanical gunlocks used for firing the ship's guns.

Skilled in working metal, the armourer likewise acted as the ship's blacksmith and 'fitter', working at the ship's portable forge, making repairs to iron components throughout the ship, manufacturing hinges, nails and bolts, and other forged work. He also had the skill to repair gunlocks, padlocks and door locks.

Cepell's armourer's mates were 37-year-old Jonathan Milebury (recorded as being Swedish) and 25-year-old Hugh Stevens. Cepell was not responsible for the weapons held by the marines.

## The ship's cook

Charles Carroll was the *Victory's* cook: '*No person is to be rated Cook who is not appointed from the Commissioners of the Navy, to entitle him to which he must be a Pensioner of the Chest at Greenwich.*' Although such men had limited culinary abilities other than boiling or roasting food, the main reason he was given junior warrant officer status relates to his responsibility for looking after the one major fire hazard on board ship, the galley stove. He was '*to have charge of the steep tub*' and see that it is '*at all times secured*'. Should it be lost overboard or by '*accident*' *which he could not prevent, he is to obtain from the Captain a certificate of the manner in which it was lost and is to make oath to the number of pieces of meat that were lost in it , that they may be allowed to the Purser's in his accounts.*' Not only was he to ensure that salt meat was properly watered steeped (to reduce the brine he also had to make sure that all provisions were '*very carefully and cleanly boiled.*'

Art. VI states: '*When fresh meat is served he is to be attentive in seeing the greens, and all other vegetables that are to be boiled with it, very carefully washed before they are put into the coppers* {boiling cauldrons] *and when he serves out soup or burgoo* [porridge] *he is strictly charged to*' dish it out equally with impartiality. He was '*not on any account to give the skimmings* [colloquially called 'slush'] *of the coppers in which salt meat has been boiled to the men either to mix with their puddings or to use in any other of manner as scarcely any thing more unwholesome, or more likely to produce the scurvy can be eaten*'.

The cook had to ensure that the coppers were thoroughly cleaned after use and '*examine them every morning before any provisions are put into them, and to inform the Mate of the watch when he has done so, who is himself to examine them and report their condition to the Lieutenant of the watch.* On the matter of fuel (coal or wood) for the galley the cook '*is to be very careful of the fuel, never using more than is really necessary under the coppers, nor allowing more fire than is wanted to be made in the range*'.

## The sailmaker and the ropemaker

Both received their warrant from the commissioners of the Navy and were directly responsible to the boatswain. Before either was allowed to receive wages each were '*required to produce a certificate signed by the Captain, of his having been sober, obedient and attentive to his work*'.

The sailmaker William Smith, aged 31, was to '*very carefully examine the sails as they are received on board and, is to inform the Boatswain if he discovers any defects in them, or any mistake in their number or dimensions. He is also to examine very carefully whether they be perfectly dry when they are put into the sail-room, that if any part of them be damp, the first opportunity may be taken to dry them*'.

Besides ensuring all sails were given wooden tallies tallied for immediate identification, the sailmaker was '*to inspect frequently the condition of the sails in the sail-rooms, to see that they are not injured by leaks or vermin,*' and he is to report to the Boatswain whenever it shall be necessary to have them taken upon deck be dried: he is to repair them whenever they require it, and to use his best endeavors to keep them always fit for service'. The sailmaker was assisted by a number of sailmaker's mates.

The ropemaker was James Hartnell, aged 27, who had to make rope of every description, and '*to adapt the rope-yarn for such kind of rope as it may be most fit. To deliver to the Boatswain all the rope and spunyarn and report the quantity they make to the Master*'.

## The surgeon [see also Chapter 16]

*Victory*'s surgeon in 1805 was Irishman William Beatty who, born in Derry (today Londonderry), studied medicine at the University of Glasgow before joining the Royal Navy as a surgeon's mate in 1791 at the age of 18. After serving in HMS *Dictator* and HMS *Hermione,* he was appointed acting-surgeon of the armed schooner HMS *Flying Fish.* Now experienced, Beatty sat for examination by the Company of Surgeons on 19 February 1795 and qualified to serve as a ship's surgeon. He then served in the *Alligator, Pomona, Amethyst, Alcmene, Resistance,* and *Spencer.* At the age of 31 he was appointed into the *Victory* in December 1804. His overall responsibilities lay with the general health of the entire ship's company, attending to their day-to-day injuries and ailments, performing operations, combating potential diseases such as scurvy, typhus and malaria, dealing with battle casualties, and the management of the ship's sick berth. Beatty's pay at the time was about £200 15s. 0d. per annum.

Most naval surgeons had great aptitude. This is not measured by the fact that most could amputate a limb and close the wound within two minutes; it was in their daily battle to keep overcrowded ships free from contagious disorders and dealing with tropical disease by using what was effectively homeopathic medicine, for which they should be credited. It is often forgotten that naval surgeons spent much time at sea, many miles from any safe or friendly harbour and, being so isolated, they acted very much on their own wits and adapted themselves to every conceivable situation that presented itself.

After Trafalgar, Beatty was appointed Physician of the Channel Fleet on 25 September 1806. He then obtained two further degrees in medicine, from the University of Aberdeen (28 February 1806), and the University of St Andrews (14 October 1817). Knighted for his services in 1831, Sir William Beatty MD FRS became the preferred physician of King William IV, the King having once been a sea officer and early friend of Nelson.

## The master-at-arms and ship's corporals

Appointed by warrant from the Admiralty, the Articles state of the master-at-arms that '*Captains are never to recommend any man who is not perfectly sober, orderly, respectful and obedient; who has not served considerable time in His Majesty's Navy, is well acquainted with ITS discipline*'.

One of the master-at-arms' main duties was '*to exercise the seamen at small arms*'. He was also '*to see the fire, and all lights (except those which the Captain shall expressively allow) extinguished at the time the Captain shall direct*' (usually at 8pm at the start of the first watch of the night when most men not on watch turned into their hammocks). The regulations also instructed him check that no lights were burning in the orlop cable tiers, cockpits and store rooms and prevent any men, '*smoking [sic] except in the galley*'. Policing good order he also had '*to prevent or put an end to, all improper drinking, and quarreling, rioting, or other disturbances*'. Offenders found were sent before the officer of the watch, confinement and subsequent punishment followed next day.

Ship's corporals, chosen on similar merit, undertook identical duties during their respective watches, under the direction of the master-at-arms.

# 5

# LIVING IN THE SHIP

What was life at sea really like in the Georgian Navy? From a twenty-first-century perspective it may appear that life in Georgian naval vessels could be an experience of great hardship, controlled by an intolerant organisation that administered cruel retribution at every opportunity. Life at sea will never be as easy or comfortable as that on land. In principle this fact applies just as much today as to the *Victory* circa 1804–05. However, excluding the ships themselves and man's mastery of seamanship, the limitations of the mariner are governed by three principal needs: the ability to sleep, adequate provisions and maintenance of health.

## ACCOMMODATION

Regardless of rank or privilege, seaman and marines all endured damp, cold and cramped conditions that alternated with a stifling environment below deck in warmer climates. Despite the many advances and improvements that would be made in later warships, circumstances changed little until the late 1960s. All of the *Victory's* commissioned officers lived in the after part of the ship; the relatively spacious quarters of the admiral and captain being subdivided, with wooden panelled bulkheads forming a day cabin, bedplace and dining cabin. The remaining lieutenants lived in segregated cabins divided off from a centrally placed wardroom with simple wood or canvas screens; the wardroom being their communal dining cabin. Regardless of material make-up, all subdivision bulkheads, transverse or longitudinally placed, could be rapidly removed when clearing the ship's gun decks for action. Whatever their rank, all officers slept in canvas or wooden-framed cots suspended from the overhead deck beams, with each man providing their own bedding.

### The senior warrant officers

The living quarters of the senior warrant officers were the least cramped on the ship. The master lived in a wood-panelled cabin under the poop deck adjacent to the captain, and as this was relatively exposed it would have been quite damp in heavy seas. The other warrant officers lived on the orlop below the lower gun deck. As their quarters did not need to be removed when clearing the ship for action they had fitted bunks. The surgeon and purser lived either side of the after cockpit of the orlop; the carpenter, boatswain either side of the fore cockpit. The gunner slept in a canvas cot within a segregated canvas cabin on the starboard side of the gunroom at the aftermost end of the lower gun deck. This room was shared with the junior marine lieutenants and the chaplain.

## The midshipmen
The more senior 'oldsters' berthed and messed in the after cockpit or in the larboard and starboard 'wings' of the orlop, all sleeping in hammock or cots. The junior midshipmen or 'youngsters' berthed and messed in the gunroom under the watchful eye of the gunner.

## Sleeping quarters
Most of the seamen forming the ship's company slept in hammocks ranged throughout the lower gun deck, the petty officers generally sleeping closer to the ship's side; in all, some 480 men. Hammocks were supplied from the purser together with a ticking mattress filled with flock, a coarse woollen blanket and a simple ticking bolster. All messed at tables that were slung between the guns, with additional tables slung in the available spaces between the rear of the guns and the hatchways capstans and miscellaneous fittings ranged along the along the centreline. Each table comprised two messes of four men, with 73 tables seating a total of 580 men in one sitting. The marines messed and berthed on the middle gun deck in similar fashion, together with the various supernumeraries, supply and secretariat ratings. Both accommodation decks were heated with portable stoves.

# PROVISIONS
There is a common misconception that victualling and diet in the Georgian Navy was poor. In reality, seamen serving in the *Victory* generally fared far better than their civilian counterparts. Working a sailing man-of-war with little or no mechanical aids was a highly labour-intensive occupation and the daily diet for each crew member needed to contain between 4500 and 5000 calories;

farm labourers would have consumed a similar figure, especially during harvest season. No professional commanding officer would expect his ship to run efficiently if his crew were undernourished with poor-quality food. The fact that the Georgian Navy was well provisioned is well supported by many examples from surviving ship's logbooks. The diet was monotonous, but this was due to the fact that only certain provisions could be carried at sea for long periods without deterioration.

## Mealtimes and allowances

The men of the *Victory* received three meals daily. Breakfast was oatmeal gruel, dinner (served at noon) stewed meat with oatmeal, peas or vegetables and supper (served around 4pm) would be cheese or butter with biscuits. General allowances per week were as follows:

| Standard rations per man | | | | | | | | |
|---|---|---|---|---|---|---|---|---|
| | Bread lb | Beer pints | Beef lb | Pork lb | Pease pints | Oatmeal pints | Butter ounces | Cheese ounces |
| Sunday | 1 | 8 | | 1 | ½ | | | |
| Monday | 1 | 8 | | | | 1 | 2 | 4 |
| Tuesday | 1 | 8 | 2 | | | | | |
| Wednesday | 1 | 8 | | | ½ | 1 | 2 | 4 |
| Thursday | 1 | 8 | | 1 | ½ | | | |
| Friday | 1 | 8 | | | ½ | 1 | 2 | 4 |
| Saturday | 1 | 8 | 2 | | | | | |
| Weekly total | 7 | 56 | 4 | 2 | 2 | 3 | 6 | 12 |

## General provisioning

When storing the *Victory* for sea these basic commodities were embarked.

| | tons (long) | lb | tonnes | kg |
|---|---|---|---|---|
| Beef and pork | 30 | 67,200 | 30.50 | 30,500 |
| Bread (hardtack biscuit) | 45 | 10,080 | 45.70 | 45,700 |
| Flour | 10 | 22,400 | 11.60 | 11,600 |
| Peas | 15 | 33,600 | 15.25 | 15,250 |
| Butter | 2 | 4,480 | 2.32 | 20,320 |

As no figure is given for oats it is likely that this formed a proportion of the flour carried, certain staple cereals being interchangeable. Beef and pork were preserved in salt and carried in casks. Suffolk cheese was generally preferred. This cheese, introduced into the navy by the Victualling Board in 1756, was chosen because its inherent natural salt content made it relatively hard and it kept better at sea. Bread comprised hard biscuit of about 1lb in weight, baked twice during manufacture, for durability, and this kept well at sea. If hardtack became damp it could become infested with weevils, the eggs of which were naturally inherent within the flour from which it was baked.

To maintain a varied healthier diet the standard provisions listed above were supplemented with beans, suet, raisins, onions, fresh vegetables, molasses or sugar. Fresh vegetables were procured whenever a ship was close to land. Also procured at every opportunity were lemons, limes and oranges; their high vitamin C content made them an ideal anti-scorbutic with which to combat scurvy.

All dried provisions, bread, biscuit, flour and oats, were stowed in the bread room located beyond the after platform of the orlop. The entire compartment, which extends downward from just below the gun deck to the lower part of the after hold, was lined with tin to keep the contents dry.

## Drink

The *Victory* had the capacity to carry the following.

|  | Tons (long) | lb | gallons | pints | tonnes | kg | litres |
|---|---|---|---|---|---|---|---|
| Water | 300 | 672,000 | 67,200 | 537,600 | 304.80 | 304,800 | 305,491.2 |
| Beer | 50 | 112,000 | 11,200 | 89,600 | 50.80 | 5.080 | 50,915.2 |

Water was carried in large barrels called 'leaguers', each containing 150 gallons of water. If storing for six months with 300 tons of water, some 450 leaguers were required. Although every man would probably consume a pint per day mixed with his ration of rum, the galley required some 520 gallons of water daily to produce breakfast and dinner. This does not account for the quantities used for steeping meat to reduce its salt content before cooking. As water consumption was quite high, it was monitored and recorded in the Master's log daily.

Water did not keep well at sea and ships replenished at every opportunity, either by sending the empty leaguers ashore in boats to refill or taking in fresh water from victualling transports accompanying the fleet. As each full leaguer weighed two-thirds of a ton, embarking water into the hold was heavy work. Accessing the hold for loading was made easier by removing the short length portable planks that formed the flat of the orlop deck together with their minor deck supports of carling and ledges.

### Beer and wine

Far safer than water, beer was universally consumed by men, women and children on land. Because of its alcohol content, beer kept far better at sea than water. Given that the *Victory* carried 50 tons of beer and that her complement of 820 men each received a daily ration of a gallon (8 pints or 4.5 litres) the entire 50 tons of beer could be consumed in two weeks. Like water, beer was replenished as often as possible from accompanying transports.

When the *Victory* was deployed with Nelson in the Mediterranean where beer or ale was a scarce commodity, the men received a daily allowance of a pint of red wine mixed with a pint of water, the wine generally the Sicilian wine Marsala. Nelson had passed through the port of Marsala in his 80-gun flagship *Foudroyant* in 1800 and introduced Marsala wine as an alternative to beer, ordering 500 barrels to take along with him to his fleet in Malta. When dark red wine became commonly used in Royal Navy ships serving in the Mediterranean the seamen nicknamed it 'black jack'. The term was then extended to refer to a deployment in the Mediterranean as being 'black jacked'.

Although the *Victory* was fitted with a segregated fish room in the after hold dried fish had not been carried in Royal Navy warships since the Seven Years' War, as it deteriorated fast. This room was often used for additional stores of beer or wine.

### Vinegar and spirits

Vinegar and spirits of wine were carried for various uses: as a disinfectant and also mixed with gunpowder for manufacturing quill firing tubes for the guns.

The *Victory* also carried spirits, mainly rum and brandy, and some Plymouth gin stowed in the spirit room in the after hold. These fluids being relatively inflammatory, this compartment was lined with fireproof plaster.

When beer was not available, each man was substituted with a daily issue of a pint of wine or half a pint of spirits, the most common being rum, procured as a byproduct from the British West Indies sugar plantations. Originally issued neat (57 per cent ABV), this had a debilitating effect on the men, the resulting drunkenness proving detrimental to both their capability and discipline.

To eradicate this problem the practice of compulsorily diluting rum in the proportion of half a pint to one quart of water (1:4) was introduced by Admiral Edward Vernon in the 1741. Vernon was nicknamed 'Old Grog' because of his habit of wearing a grogram cloak (a waterproof fabric comprising a mix of silk and wool) and the diluted rum issue became known as 'grog'.

Furthermore the ration was also split into two issues, one between 10am and noon and the other between 4pm and 6pm. In 1756 Navy regulations required adding small quantities of lemon or lime juice to the ration to prevent scurvy.

## VICTUALLING

Naval warships such as the *Victory* often replenished from the land or from accompanying victualling ships. For example, while deployed off Toulon between 1 and 5 August 1803 the *Victory* received from the *Isabella* transport a total of 87½ tons of water, 11 bullocks, 5730lb onions and 2070 lemons. Anchored for nine days in the Sound off Maddalena, between Corsica and Sardinia, in November 1803, Captain Hardy records that the *Victory* embarked 83 tons of water and various provisions comprising '*397 bags of Bread 7 casks of beef & Dº. of Pork 3 of Flour 3 of oatmeal*'; also taken on were 10 live bullocks '*Weighing when killed 2422 lbs*', and 38 tons of water.

Storing again on 23 November, the *Victory* received '*on Board 1293 lbs of Lemon Juice in 17 Cases 4 barrels of Sugar containing 1641 lbs from HMS* Excellent *also 1 butt of small beer*' and on 22 December, the *Victory* embarked 165 bags of bread and after anchoring in Agincourt sound Saturday 24 December *Victory's* log records; '*received 'Boatswains Stores & 22 Pipes of Wine from the Transports*'. Embarked the following day: '*61 Pipes of Wine 30 Casks of Beef 32 Casks Pork 18 of Oatmeal 3 of Rice and 6 of Suet from the* Eliza *transport*'. On 10 January 1804, the *Victory* received '*bullocks weighing 1,711 pounds, and seven bags of onions weighing 814 pounds*' from the *Seahorse*. Provisioning again on Thursday 19 January, the ship embarked '*3 Puncheons of Rum containing 253 Gallons & 14 Puncheons of Brandy containing 1220 Gallons from HMS* Canopus.'

Particularly noteworthy is that warships are replenishing each other's stores. Using the journals of Nelson's former flagship, the 80-gun *Foudroyant*, as another example, when operating off Rio de Janeiro in May 1808 she embarked a wide variety of foodstuffs influenced by locality, including oranges as a vitamin C substitute for lemons and limes.

| Foodstuff | Weight/volume | |
|---|---|---|
| | Imperial | Metric |
| Bread | 31,360lb | 14,112.0kg |
| Coffee | 2,988lb | 1,344.6kg |
| Flour | 1,752lb | 788.4kg |
| Fresh beef | 1,380lb | 621.0kg |
| Pease (97 bushels) | 5,432lb | 2,444.4kg |
| Rice | 643lb | 289.4kg |
| Sugar | 4,470lb | 2,911.5kg |
| Oranges (7,680 fruit) | 3,360lb | 1,512kg |
| Vegetables | 2,240lb | 1,008.0kg |
| Wine (37 casks) | 3,885 gallons | 17,649.6 litres |
| Wine (possibly in 6 casks) | 634 gallons | 2,880.3 litres |
| Estimated total weight | 44.14 tons | 44.85 tonnes |

# 6

# CONDITIONS OF SERVICE

## THE ARTICLES OF WAR

All men serving in the Georgian Navy worked to a strict code of ethical rules called the *Articles of War*. These provided all officers commanding a King's ship supreme autonomy over the subjects of his crew and the running of his ship. When assuming command and commissioning a ship into service it was common practice for the captain to read out the *Articles of War* to the entire ship's company. This act was usually repeated weekly after the Sunday divine service to ensure that discipline was maintained.

Not to be confused with punishment, discipline is the practice applied to attain good authoritative organisation. Admiral Collingwood's statement '*Nothing is achieved without order or discipline*' encapsulates the essential requirements of ship management. Any breakdown of order or discipline could result in the total loss of the ship, damage or loss of equipment, unnecessary injury or death, or the failure to engage an enemy. Punishment, the means to maintain that order and discipline, was readily accepted by officers and seamen alike under the authority of the aforesaid *Articles of War*. Matters of discipline were further supported by the *Regulations and Instructions relating to His Majesty's Service at Sea*, contained in a 440-page volume that laid out the duties and responsibilities for all rank and rates personnel within the Royal Navy or carried aboard a warship.

The first '*Act for establishing Articles and orders for the regulating and better government of His Majesty's Navies, Ships of War and Forces by Sea*' was passed in 1661 by the first Parliament of King Charles II. This laid the foundation of effective naval administration. To eliminate arising problems of discipline and operational circumstances, these rules were amended by the Board of the Admiralty under Lord Anson in 1749 and again in 1757 by the Parliament of George II. These Articles contain 36 specific regulations and laws, together with their corresponding penalties. The foremost article formally directed all commanding officers that they were to uphold the Christian religion and conduct Divine Service on Sunday. The remainder covered all points concerning failure of duty, espionage, disobedience of orders, drunkenness, desertion, not pursuing the enemy and cowardice in the face of the enemy. Besides matters such as 'false Musters' and 'wasting of stores', the Articles covered simple humane factors; i.e. *'of stripping or ill using Persons taken on board a Prize'* [ship].

The Articles also reflected the social order of the day and upheld the accepted God-fearing Christian values of the period, examples being:

Article XXVII: Murder, as on land, carried the death penalty.

Article XXVII: *'The unnatural and detestable Sin of Sodomy with Man or Beast "shall be punished by with Death by the Sentence of a Court-martial".'*

Article XXVII: Robbery, although this could be *'punished with Death'*, carried the caveat *'or otherwise, as a Court-martial, upon Consideration of circumstances, shall find meet'*. This provided the Navy the means for an alternative punishment that satisfied the need to differentiate the gravity of the crime from petty theft where sparing a life of a useful crew member was considered both morally just and practical.

## ADMIRALTY REGULATIONS AND INSTRUCTIONS

Introduced in 1787, the Admiralty *Regulations and Instructions Relating to His Majesty's Service at Sea* covered the more general day-to-day issues of management and duties of officers and personnel, such as routine, storekeeping and related accounts, including those of the purser, boatswain, gunner and carpenter. Supporting these guidelines were captain's *Standing Orders* that spelled out regulations, duties and routines that related directly to the ship in which he had command. By 1807 such orders were becoming quite standardised throughout the fleet.

## PUNISHMENT

Authority, discipline and punishment within the Georgian Navy need to be considered in the context of the period. In Georgian society, punishing an offender by flogging was not just confined to the navy or army, it was equally common on land and used on men and women alike; it was a socially acceptable form of punishment. If naval punishment was apparently so awful then why, during the Great Mutiny of 1797, did the seamen not raise this factor as a major point of grievance when petitioning the Admiralty with other demands? Although most ships involved with this mutiny were controlled by the seamen, boatswains and petty officers fully maintained discipline on the ships, meting out harsh punishment as and when was deemed necessary throughout this period of insurrection.

Most punishments were confined to flogging on the ship, the punishment being authorised by the commanding officer. Officially no captain could award more than two dozen lashes without seeking higher authority; that invariably required courts-martial. However, as the tables on pages 58 and 59 show, this was not always convenient.

Floggings, using a cat-o-nine-tails wielded by boatswain's mates, was always witnessed by the entire ship's company, the offender being tied to an upturned grating at the fore end of the quarterdeck where all could see. Marines with loaded muskets and fixed bayonets were lined up on deck to deter possible insurrection. Before punishment commenced the captain would read out the name of the offender, his charge and sentence and the relevant part of the *Articles of War* appertaining to the crime.

Although punishment was swift, decisive and in most cases just, by 1800 it was becoming common for captains to carry out punishment weekly, exploiting the event of having a number of men flogged to make a statement, rather than mustering the entire ship's company to witness one or two floggings. Furthermore, analysis shows that as the war with France was prolonged, the Admiralty and its officers were increasingly faced with crews made up of conscripts and other non-professional seamen, with the result that punishment had to be administered more frequently to maintain authority when discipline deteriorated. This does not imply that punishment became less justified but does emphasise that tolerance had lessened.

Analysing a host of ship's journals recording daily incidents and punishments, the most common offences generally relate to drunkenness, disobedience and neglect of duty, the former often leading to the other two; the *Victory* was no exception.

| Punishments given out by Captain Thomas Masterman Hardy in the Victory | | | |
|---|---|---|---|
| **Tuesday 3 July 1804** | | | |
| Name | Rate | Offence | No. of lashes |
| William Inwood | Boatswain's Mate | Theft | 48 |
| Anthony Antonio | Cook's Mate | Disobedience of Orders | 36 |
| Thomas Palmer | Seaman | Drunkenness | 36 |
| John Thomas | Seaman | Insolence & disobedience of orders | 24 |
| John Brice | Marine | Neglect of duty | 12 |
| Daniel Sweeny | Marine | Contempt & drunkenness | 36 |
| **Tuesday 10 July 1804** | | | |
| Name | Rate | Offence | No. of lashes |
| Patrick Merryan | Seaman | Drunkenness | 36 |
| Peter McGee | Seaman | Drunkenness | 36 |
| Peter Mcgee | Seaman | Drunkenness & fighting | 48 |
| Thomas Maloney | Seaman | Drunkenness & fighting | 48 |
| Samuel Baker | Marine | Sleeping at his Post | 24 |
| **Tuesday 24 July 1804** | | | |
| Name | Rate | Offence | No. of lashes |
| Patrick Merryan | Seaman | Drunkenness | 36 |
| Henry Butcher | Seaman | Theft | 48 |
| Joseph Brown | Seaman | Insolence | 24 |
| John Jacobs | Seaman | Fighting | 24 |
| John Brown | Seaman | Drunkenness | 24 |
| Thomas Thomas | Seaman | Fighting | 12 |
| Henry Thompson | Seaman | Fighting | 24 |
| John Thomas | Seaman | Insolence and disobeying orders | 24 |

The most telling example relates to the period in the *Victory* just before the Battle of Trafalgar:

| Punishment given out by Captain Thomas Masterman Hardy in the Victory | | | |
|---|---|---|---|
| **Saturday 19 October 1805** | | | |
| Name | Rate | Offence | No. of lashes |
| James Dennington | Seaman | Drunkenness | 36 |
| John Dunkin | Seaman | Drunkenness | 36 |
| James Evans | Seaman | Drunkenness | 36 |
| John Hall | Seaman | Drunkenness | 36 |
| James Mansfield | Seaman | Drunkenness | 36 |
| John Murphy | Seaman | Drunkenness | 36 |
| William Pritchard | Seaman | Drunkenness | 36 |
| William Skinner | Seaman | Drunkenness | 36 |
| Henry Stiles | Seaman | Drunkenness | 36 |
| William Wood (3$^{rd}$) | Seaman | Drunkenness | 36 |
| Notes:<br>1. Despite suffering the lash all 10 would be fighting at Trafalgar two days later.<br>2. William Skinner would be killed in the action two days later. | | | |

One crime not tolerated was theft which, because it affected morale and trust among the crew, carried greater punishment. Petty theft was usually dealt with by 'running the gauntlet' where the offender was forced to pass between two rows of seamen who systematically beat him with a rope's end – a punishment considered to be quite effective.

Other typical crimes recorded include: fighting, leaving the boat on duty and neglect of duty. The number of lashes given was generally 12 to 24. Wider analysis shows that men were often flogged for lesser anti-social offences: '*mutinous expressions*', or '*uncleanliness*' for example. The former probably relates to any expression of contempt, the latter generally to failure to wash the body or clothes. In such cases, the numbers of lashes given ranged between six and 12. Like all groups in society, there are always the minorities who consistently flaunt the rules and no matter how often they are punished, they continuously disobey. Extant logbooks clearly show names of repeat offenders.

Records also show of discipline deteriorating according to situation. These include ships on constant blockade duty with boredom being the main contributory factor; problems arising in the aftermath of close action. After the Battle of Copenhagen on 1 April 1801, three marines serving in HMS *Raisonable* were flogged with 24 lashes for '*mutinous behaviour*'.

Location also affected punishment and it was commonly found that discipline appeared to break down when the ship was not at sea. This was primarily because the seamen were not in sea watches and were therefore less occupied. Marines tended to be more problematic at sea than when more actively employed in harbour. Drunkenness created continuous problems: one man in the *Victory* received '*Eighteen lashes for Drunkenness, cutting down a Man in his Hammock and beating him*'. Although flogging was finally abolished in 1876, the punishment has not been officially rescinded in the Royal Navy.

## THE DEATH PENALTY AND SERIOUS OFFENCES

Offences carrying a death penalty, imprisonment, dismissal from the service or floggings of more than three dozen ashes were dealt with by a courts-martial. This comprised a minimum of five senior officers and admirals to try the defendant who, under these circumstances, could have counsel. Although logbooks show that courts-martial were held quite often, offenders were not always found guilty; in fact, most were acquitted because of mitigating circumstances.

While most senior officers were executed by a firing squad, the death penalty for petty officers, seamen and marines was hanging. This was always carried out on the ships to which they belonged, the physical part of the execution being carried out by their fellow men. Prior to the execution a gun was fired calling for an officer from each ship to witness the event, the officer concerned embarking in a boat '*manned and armed*'. The ship's companies of every ship in the squadron were likewise called to their decks to witness the affair.

His head covered with a hood, the victim stood on the larboard (port) side cathead with the noose around his neck ready. Signalled by a second gun, some 20 seamen ran aft with the rope and '*hoisted the man into eternity*' from the block hanging at the yard-arm of the fore lower yard where it remained for an hour before being lowered.

Second to hanging was flogging around the fleet, whereby a man could be given between 100 and 500 lashes. Tied to two capstan bars erected in a boat, the unfortunate victim was rowed from ship to ship in the squadron, receiving a number of lashes at each ship. In the boat were officers and armed marines from the offender's ship, plus a drummer who played a 'rogue's march'. Also in the boat was a surgeon who would stop the punishment if the victim's life seemed threatened. Under these circumstances, the remainder of the punishment would be deferred until the man was medically fit enough to receive the outstanding number of lashes. It was not uncommon for some men to die from this punishment. Sentences of this type generally applied to deserters who had insufficient mitigating circumstances.

## PAY

Though less than that earned in the merchant service, Royal Navy pay was at least reliable, although often paid in arrears or when the ship was 'paid off' out of service. Approximate examples of pay for those serving in a first-rate ship such as the *Victory* are given below:

| Approximate pay scales in the Victory | | | | |
| --- | --- | --- | --- | --- |
| Group rank or rate | £ | Shillings (s) | Pence (d) | Period |
| Captain | 32 | 4 | 0 | Monthly |
| Lieutenant | 8 | 8 | 0 | Monthly |
| Master | 12 | 8 | 0 | Monthly |
| Chaplain | 150 | 0 | 0 | Annually |
| Surgeon | 0 | 11 | 0 | Daily |
| Carpenter | 6 | 16 | 6 | Monthly |
| Gunner | 4 | 16 | 0 | Monthly |
| Purser | 47 | 2 | 0 | Annually |
| Boatswain | 4 | 16 | 0 | Monthly |
| Sailmakers and ropemakers | 1 | 18 | 6 | Monthly |
| Petty officers | 2 | 2 | 6 | Monthly |
| Carpenter's crew | 2 | 16 | 0 | Monthly |
| Gunner's mates and quarter gunners | 1 | 16 | 6 | Monthly |
| Quartermasters and mates | 2 | 0 | 6 | Monthly |
| Cook | 1 | 8 | 0 | Monthly |

| Able seaman | 1 | 15 | 0 | Monthly |
| Ordinary seamen | 1 | 5 | 0 | Monthly |
| Marine sergeants | 1 | 15 | 0 | Monthly |
| Marine privates | | 5 | 0 | Monthly |
| Midshipmen | 1 | 15 | 0 | Monthly |

1. The chaplain received 1 groat (4d) per head of men in the ship; i.e. his parish.
2. At 11 shillings per day, this puts the surgeon on approximately £17.10s per month, reflecting both his responsibility and academic abilities.
3. This wage is comparable to a common labourer.

Although the pay did not fully reflect the realistic hardships of serving in the King's ships, the likelihood of receiving prize money added a great incentive.

## Prize money

This practice, first introduced by law under the Cruisers and Convoys Act of 1708, was a monetary reward paid out to a ship's crew for capturing or sinking an enemy vessel the claiming of which was usually heard in an Admiralty prize court. All captured ships were evaluated by a prize agent who made his assessment based on the ship's hull, masts, rigging and sails, together with her guns, stores and other equipment. This collective sum, divided into eighths, was distributed as follows: Two eighths of the prize money went to the captain. One eighth of the money went to the admiral or commander-in-chief who signed the ship's written orders. However, if the orders came direct from the Admiralty in Whitehall this eighth also went directly to the captain. One eighth was divided among the lieutenants, the master and the captain of marines (if carried). The next eighth was divided among the wardroom warrant officers (the surgeon, purser and chaplain), together with the standing officers (the gunner, boatswain and carpenter). This same share was also given out to the master's mates and lieutenants of marines. Another eighth was divided among the junior warrant and petty officers, their mates, the sergeants of marines, captain's clerk, surgeon's mates, and the midshipmen. The final two eighths were distributed among the crew: the able and ordinary seamen, specialist seamen, landsmen, boys and marine privates.

The greatest amount of prize money awarded relates to the capture of the Spanish frigate *Hermione* on 31 May 1762 by HMS *Active* and HMS *Favourite*. The two British captains each received about £65,000, the seamen and marines got £482–£485 per man. Another example was the capture of the two Spanish ships, *Thetis* and *Santa Brigida*, by the British frigates *Naiad* and *Ethalion* off the Spanish naval port of Vigo in October 1799. They were carrying silver specie and luxury trade goods. Both captured ships were taken to Britain and their combined cargoes were valued at £652,000. Prize money awarded was distributed among the crews of four British frigates deployed off Vigo, each captain receiving £40,730 and each of the seamen getting £182 4s 9¾d, the equivalent of 10 years' pay.

## Trafalgar prize money

While Trafalgar may have been a glorious victory with many enemy vessels captured, most of the prize ships taken were lost in the terrible storm following the battle. Despite the dangers of the storm some Spanish ships were actually rescued by a daring Spanish commander. Some British prize crews, unable to handle the battle-wrecked ships, resorted to handing them over to their French crews to jointly battle the danger. Other damaged prize ships simply foundered. In short, there was very little prize money to distribute among the ships of Nelson's fleet. When the *Victory's* crew received their prize money on 10 April 1807 it was divided as follows:

| Class | Group rank or rate | £ | Shillings (s) | Pence (d) |
|-------|--------------------|----|---------------|-----------|
| 1st | Captain | 973 | 0 | 0 |
| 2nd | Naval lieutenants, captain of marines and master | 65 | 11 | 0 |
| 3rd | Boatswain, gunner, surgeon, carpenter and purser | 44 | 14 | 0 |
| 3rd | Marine lieutenants, master's mates, secretary and chaplain | 44 | 14 | 0 |
| 4th | Various mates, petty officers and midshipmen | 10 | 14 | 0 |
| 4th | Assistant surgeon, yeomen and clerks | 10 | 14 | 0 |
| 5th | Master-at-arms, marine sergeants | 1 | 17 | 6 |
| 5th | Able seamen, ordinary seamen and quarter gunners | 1 | 17 | 6 |
| 5th | Marine corporals and privates | 1 | 17 | 6 |
| 5th | Landsmen, boys and supply ratings | 1 | 17 | 6 |

## Government grant money

With the loss of so many prize ships in the storm after Trafalgar, British officers and seamen lost considerable potential prize earnings. Compensating for this loss, the British government awarded a government grant which, like prize money, was distributed in five classes. When the *Victory's* crew received their government grant money on 10 April 1807 it was divided as follows:

| Class | Group rank or rate | £ | Shillings (s) | Pence (d) |
|-------|--------------------|-----|------|-----|
| 1st | Captain | 2389 | 7 | 6 |
| 2nd | Naval lieutenants, captain of marines and master | 161 | | |
| 3rd | Boatswain, gunner, surgeon, carpenter and purser | 108 | 12 | 0 |
| 3rd | Marine lieutenants, master's mates, secretary and chaplain | 108 | 12 | 0 |
| 4th | Various mates, petty officers and midshipmen | 26 | 6 | 0 |
| 4th | Assistant surgeon, yeomen and clerks | 26 | 6 | 0 |
| 5th | Master-at-arms, marine sergeants | 4 | 12 | 6 |
| 5th | Able seamen, ordinary seamen and quarter gunners | 4 | 12 | 6 |
| 5th | Marine corporals and privates | 4 | 12 | 6 |
| 5th | Landsmen, boys and supply ratings | 4 | 12 | 6 |

## Pensions

Payable on discharge from the service either through age or disability, these were provided by the Royal Greenwich Hospital to all applicants who could prove that they had served in either the Navy or Marines. This applied to those living in or out of the hospital, with those living in enjoying the facilities provided. Out-pensions were a form of superannuation in that claimants had to show former service in the Navy or Marines; however, as the pensions were scarcely sufficient to live on, these recipients were not restricted from seeking other employment to supplement their income, especially as many out-pensioners of the hospital were still relatively young men. Both in- and out-pensioners could re-enter the Navy, wherein their pensions lapsed until their later discharge.

# THE ROYAL MARINES

Introduced in 1664, the Marines were initially formed as an amphibious light infantry force of foot soldiers attached to the Royal Navy. This arrangement was officially formalised in 1755. Recognised by Admiral Sir John Jervis (Earl St Vincent) for their gallant efforts during the ensuing French Revolutionary War, the Marines were given the upgraded title of Royal Marines, with royal consent by King George III in 1802. The entire company of Royal Marines who entered into the *Victory* on 14 April 1803 came from the Chatham Division and comprised 153 men.

## MARINE OFFICERS

Their commander was Captain of Marines Charles William Adair from County Antrim, Ireland. Adair, who came from a distinguished family of marine officers, had joined the Marines as a second lieutenant of marines in 1782. His uncle was Captain William Prowse who commanded the 36-gun fifth-rate frigate HMS *Sirius* at Trafalgar. During the battle, Adair was killed by a musket ball in the back of his neck while repelling boarders.

The First Lieutenant of Marines was James Goodwin Peake from Stafford, who joined as a second lieutenant in 1796. Although wounded in the battle, Peake assumed command of the marines when Adair was killed. The second lieutenants of Marines were Lewis Roatley a Welshman from Neath Glamorganshire who entered into the *Victory* on August 1805, and Lewis Buckle Reeves from County Clare, Ireland, who was badly wounded in the action. All the Marine officers berthed within or near the wardroom and messed with the naval lieutenants and other wardroom officers.

The remaining Marines consisted of four sergeants, four corporals and 138 privates. The sergeants were Samuel Dowden from County Monaghan Ireland, Daniel Fearall from Surrey, John Gilman from County Cork, Ireland, and James Secker from Norfolk. Ironically it was Secker, a Norfolk man like Nelson, who immediately went to the Admiral's aid when Nelson was fatally shot. Although most privates were English, 15 per cent were of Irish, Scots and Welsh origin, four per cent were Italian and Maltese and one man was German. Two of the privates were drummers who would 'beat to quarters' when the ship was clearing for action and one private was a trumpeter. (The use of trumpets was a throwback from seventeenth-century battle practice).

One Irishman from Shannon killed at Trafalgar was 44-year-old Private John Brennan. (Ship's Muster Book No. M.096). His share of prize money and government grant was paid posthumously to John Wolfe of Cork for Brennan's widow Johanna on 17 July 1808.

## GENERAL DUTIES

The Marines served as a professional fighting military unit both ashore and afloat. Ashore they were an amphibious assault force attacking coastal installations and cutting-out (capturing) enemy ships at anchor. Afloat their duties were multifarious; under normal sailing conditions they were generally employed as sentinels guarding the powder rooms, magazines, the spirit room and other important store rooms. They also guarded the entrances of the admiral's and officer's quarters, protecting the ship's officers from the crew. This was particularly prevalent since the Great Mutiny of 1797 and infiltration of revolutionary Jacobin sympathisers inciting insurrection. Subsequently the rank and file of the Marines lived and berthed within the fore section of the middle gun deck, forming a 'protective barrier', between the seamen on the lower deck and the wardroom officers situated aft.

The preference for segregated berthing from seamen was mutually respected. Like the seamen, the Marines slept in hammocks and ate at tables slung between the guns or where convenient. Marines also provided general assistance to the seamen where unskilled heavy labour was required, such as hauling on ropes when the ship was manoeuvring, adding manpower to turn the capstan when weighing anchor or embarking heavy stores and guns. Marines were not obliged to work aloft and could not be ordered to do so by any officer.

Like all military units, the Royal Marines maintained their own muskets, bayonets and associated equipment. In most instances their muskets were 'bright' or polished for ceremonial needs as opposed to the black (dull) muskets maintained as 'ships weapons' under the charge of the gunner.

# IN BATTLE

When the *Victory* came into action the Marines provided extra manpower to operate the guns and small arms fire and created a disciplined defence at close quarters using bayonet and half pikes to repel boarders. They were also proficient at throwing grenades. It was practice to station Marines up in the fore, main and mizzen tops, with their muskets acting as snipers to pick off enemy officers to break down command. While this could be advantageous, Nelson disapproved; a previous experience at the Battle of Hyères Islands in July 1795 had shown him the danger of cartridges and potential musket flash fire in the rigging; fire had broken out in the foretop of the French ship *Alcide* which, engulfed in flames, was consumed by an explosion half an hour later, causing the loss of about 300 crew.

The Marines also assisted the gun crews. Recording the battle scenes during Trafalgar, Lieutenant of Marines Roatley wrote: '*Between decks looked like the infernal regions of hell; the marines had cast of their scarlet jackets and in their checked shirts and white trousers there was no distinction between marine and seamen and all were working like horses.*'

# 8

# LEARNING THE ROPES

## SEAMANSHIP IN THE AGE OF SAIL

Seamanship is the art of controlling the ship, her rigging and sails in absolute safety and it is the fundamental means to survival in the hostile environment of the sea and respective wind and weather conditions. It also applies to the competent operation of cables and anchors, collectively termed as ground tackle (because of their association with the seabed), and of the ship's boats. Another part of seamanship relates to the intricate practice of tying knots, bends and hitches, splicing ropes together and running ropes through sets of pulley blocks, the blocks providing mechanical advantage (a purchase) to haul, raise, or turn yards, hoist or lower sails and generally manoeuvre or raise heavy loads or carry or dissipate strain incurred as required. All three aspects of seamanship are covered in the next three chapters

## *VICTORY'S* SAILS

The maximum number of sails that could be set on the *Victory* was 37, including her staysails and studdingsails. This vast amount of canvas gave her a sail area of 6510 square yards (5468 square metres), an area one third greater than the size of a football pitch. It was very unlikely that all her sails would be set at the same time. According to the boatswain's store muster for March 1805, a total of 59 sails (including spares) were carried on the ship.

*Victory's* fastest recorded speed was 11 knots (12.5mph). With her entire spread of 37 sails at an area of 58,590 square feet, the power generated in a force 5 wind amounted to some 2,343.6 horsepower. This is compatible with the Italian square-rigged training ship *Amerigo Vespuccio*, a ship of 4000 tons launched in 1931, which has 23 sails, generating 904 horsepower.

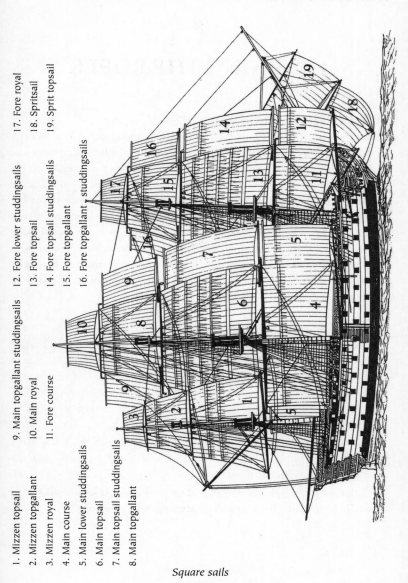

1. Mizzen topsail
2. Mizzen topgallant
3. Mizzen royal
4. Main course
5. Main lower studdingsails
6. Main topsail
7. Main topsail studdingsails
8. Main topgallant

9. Main topgallant studdingsails
10. Main royal
11. Fore course
12. Fore lower studdingsails
13. Fore topsail
14. Fore topsail studdingsails
15. Fore topgallant
16. Fore topgallant studdingsails

17. Fore royal
18. Spritsail
19. Sprit topsail

*Square sails*

8. Main topgallant staysail
9. Fore staysail
10. Fore topmast staysail
11. Jib
12. Flying jib

1. Mizzen (spanker)
2. Mizzen staysail
3. Mizzen topmast staysail
4. Mizzen topgallant staysail
5. Main staysail
6. .Main topmast staysail
7. Middle staysail

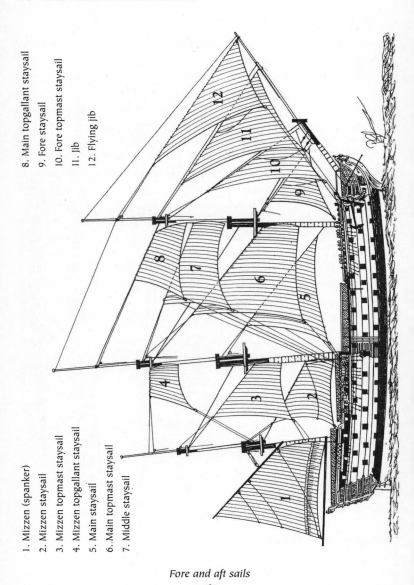

*Fore and aft sails*

## SHIP HANDLING

Operating and manoeuvring a large three-decked ship under sail in variable conditions required considerable skill, with many people working in teams responsible to each single mast and bowsprit. A three-decked ship such as the *Victory* differs little from any other ship-rigged vessel: a three-masted vessel with a bowsprit, having square sails attached to horizontal yards set on all masts, together with fore and aft sails set on rope stays running between the masts. This applied to any two-decked 74-gun ship or a single-decked frigate such as HMS *Trincomalee* (1817). Despite the physical differences in size of the rig, masts, yards, sail area and number of sails, the fundamental principles remained identical, as each ship-rigged vessel required some 728 blocks to operate the rig. The locations from where operating ropes were handled and secured were virtually universal: A seaman taken out of the *Victory* would know where the fore topgallant leech line fall was belayed in HMS *Unicorn* (1824) or the American heavy 44-gun frigate USS *Constitution*.

Besides having a competent master and boatswain, along with the assistant boatswain's mates, the crew needed a lot of training to get the teams dedicated to each mast working together to execute sailing manoeuvres swiftly. Capable topmen were needed to handle sails aloft in all weathers both night and day.

### Handling sails

Only the basic principles of major evolutions in sail handling are provided in the following section:

1. Setting or taking in sails
2. Tacking ship
3. Wearing ship
4. Heaving to
5. Reefing sails
6. Getting the ship under sail from being at anchor
7. Bringing the ship to anchor
8. Sailing performance.

### Setting or taking in sails

Each type of sail, whether square, triangular or quadrilateral, was operated by dedicated ropes, each of which served a specific control function. In most cases, these ropes could be operated from the deck without needing men to go aloft to enable easy and quick response in sail handling under any circumstances.

## Square sails

Regardless of mast or yards, these were all basically controlled or operated by the following ropes:

| Control ropes for the square sails | | |
|---|---|---|
| Rope name | No. rigged | Function |
| Sheets | 2 | Hold down and hold out the outer lower corners of sail |
| Tacks | 2 | Hold down outer lower corners of course sails only |
| Clewlines | 2 | Haul up the outer lower corners of sail into its yard |
| Buntlines | 3–4 | Haul up the foot or bunt of the sail to its yard |
| Leechlines | 2 | Haul up the leech or bunt of the sail into its yard |
| Bowlines | 2 | Hold out and haul forward the leeches of the sail to windward |

## Fore and aft triangular staysails and jib sails

Regardless of masts, these were all controlled or operated by the following ropes:

| Control ropes for triangular staysails and jib sails | | |
|---|---|---|
| Rope name | No. rigged | Function |
| Sheets | 2 | Hold down and out the after lower corners of sail |
| Tacks | 1 | Hold down the fore lower corners of sail |
| Halliards | 1 | Hoist up the sail on its stay |
| Downhaulers | 1 | Haul down the sail |
| Outhauler | 1 | Haul out the fore corner of sail (jib sails only) |
| Inhauler | 1 | Haul in the sail (jib sails only) |

## Fore and aft quadrilateral mizzen sail

Alternatively known as the driver (and in the mercantile fleet the spanker), this sail was controlled or operated by the following ropes:

| Control ropes for the quadrilateral mizzen sail | | |
|---|---|---|
| Rope name | No. rigged | Function |
| Sheets | 2 | Hold down and haul out the after lower corner of sail |
| Tacks | 1 | Hold down the fore lower corner of sail |
| Brails | 3 | Hoist in and haul up the sail to its mast and gaff yard |

## Studding or stunsails

In additon to the above, the *Victory* had studding or stunsails. Also called steering sails, these were used in very light winds. All stunsails were actually bent (secured) to their individual yards which were hoisted and suspended from horizontal stunsail booms that were run out beyond the yard arms of the course, and topsail yards. Topgallant stunsails simply ran up to the eye at the topgallant yardarm. All individual sails had tacks and sheets that functioned in the same way as those mentioned earlier.

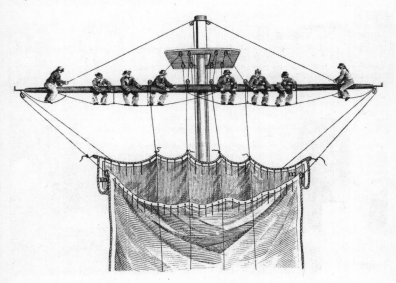

*All sails had to be hoisted by hand and bent to their respective
yards by means of rope lacings called robbands*

*Left: The lower masts were transversely supported by 11-inch rope shrouds indirectly secured to the ships side with pairs of wooden deadeyes laced together with lanyards.*

*Below: The Victory was rigged with 27 miles of hemp rope and 728 wooden pulley blocks.*

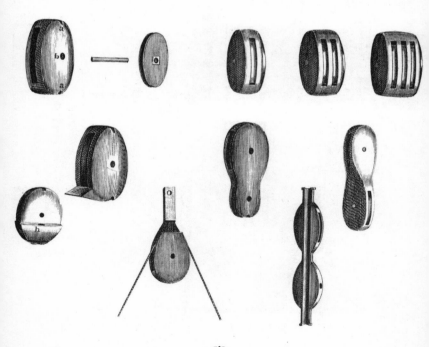

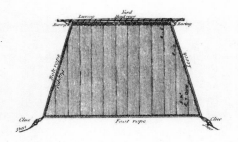

*Main topsail and yard*

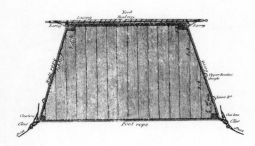

*Main topgallant sail
and yard*

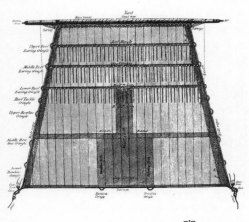

*Main royal sail and yard*

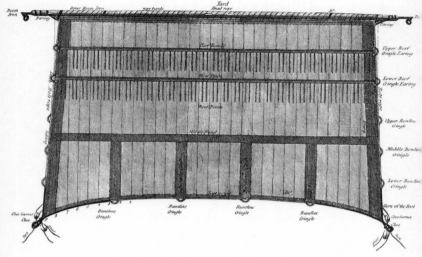

*Main course sail and yard*

## Tacking ship

Unlike modern yachts which have fore- and aft-rigged sails and can sail far closer to the wind (about 4 points or 46 degrees off the wind), a square-rigged ship such as the *Victory* would be extremely lucky if she could sail 6 points (69 degrees) off the wind. The only way to sail on a course against the wind is to carry out a series of zigzag courses (called tacks), with the wind prevailing first on the larboard (port) side of the ship and then on the starboard side, the ship having to turn her head through the wind at the end of each zig-zag leg in succession.

Tacking was a fast method of turning the ship through the wind on to another tack or course. It had two disadvantages:
1. It could put a lot of strain on the rigging;
2. The manoeuvre could often fail in square-rigged ships if forward momentum of the ship was lost at the crucial moment.

Before attempting to tack a square-rigged ship the vessel must have sufficient way (momentum forward) in order to turn the head through the wind. Therefore the manoeuvre must be precise and quickly executed and failure to do so will result in the ship's head falling back off the wind and not getting on to the new tack. In this situation, the ship is said to have 'missed stays'. For the purpose of the written procedure, the ship is sailing close-hauled (just off the wind) on a larboard tack – that is the wind prevailing on the larboard (port) side.

*Illustration from Darcy Lever (1819) showing the sequence of tacking ship.*

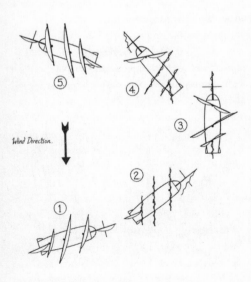

*Diagram showing the sequence of tacking ship. This involved turning the head of the ship through the wind. The diagram shows the ship close-hauled on a larboard tack, the wind coming from the larboard side.*

**1 'Stations for stays.**
*This order alerts the crew to man their stations and set the braces for running. The helm was eased to leeward (downwind) to increase the speed of the ship. Once ready, the next order 'Stand by to tack, ready about' is given.*

**2 'Helm's a lee'** *The jib sails are eased to assist the turn and, because wind is spilled by the square sails, the wind effect driving the ship is reduced.*

**3 'Hand taut, main and mizzen sail haul'.** *The yards on the main and mizzen masts are turned around quickly to the opposite side, catching some wind to drive the stem backwards. The rudder is centred once the ship slows down (loses way). The wind sets the sails 'aback', pushing the head of the ship through the wind.*

**4** *The boom of the mizzen sail or spanker is eased over the larboard, likewise the sheet jib in preparation for a starboard tack.* **'Let go and haul'.** *The fore mast yards are immediately braced round. The wind fills the sails on all three masts, mizzen sail and jib bringing it round on to a starboard tack. All ropes are coiled and secured.*

## Wearing ship

The alternative manoeuvre to tacking was wearing, which involved turning the stern of the ship through the wind. In modern terms, this manoeuvre is commonly called gybing. Wearing ship had two advantages:

1. The manoeuvre put less strain on on the rigging.

2. Wearing was an easier and more positive manoeuvre to undertake in a square-rigged ship to get on to an alternative tack or course.

The one disadvantage of wearing was that it was a far slower manoeuvre which involved more sail handling.

*Illustration from Darcy Lever (1819) showing the sequence of wearing ship.*

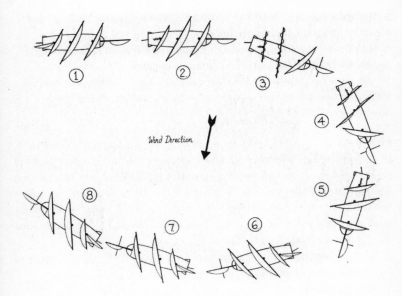

*Diagram showing the sequence of wearing ship.*

*This manoeuvre involved turning the stern of the ship through the wind. The diagram shows the ship close-hauled on a larboard tack, the wind coming from the larboard side.*

1 **'Stations for wearing ship'** *The crew to man their respective stations and prepare the braces for running. Once ready, the next order,* **'Stand by to wear ship'**, *is given.*

2 **'Up mainsail and mizzen (spanker). Brace in the after yards'** *The main course and mizzen sail are brailed (furled) up to prevent them opposing the turn.* **'Up helm'**, *the rudder turns the ship to starboard and, takes the ship's stern across the wind.*

3 **'Main and mizzen mast, let go and haul'** *The yards of the main and mizzen masts are braced round to feather the sails, allowing the wind to spill from the sails.*

4. *As the wind comes on to the starboard quarter acting on the sails of the fore mast and the headsail (jibs), the ship begins to turn.*

5 '**Square the fore sails, let go and haul**' *The fore yards are squared and the headsails are hauled over the larboard.*
6 '**Haul aboard, haul out**' *The mainsail and mizzen sail (spanker) are reset and the lee braces of the fore yards are braced round.*
7 *With the sails on the main and mizzen masts filing, the ship gathers speed.*
8 *The ship now proceeds on a starboard tack. All sails are trimmed and respective ropes coiled or secured.*

## Heaving to

In principle, a ship will 'heave to' or be 'hove to' by counter bracing round the yards in such a manner that the wind plays against the sails on one mast, setting them aback, opposing the forward drive on the sails of the other mast. As a result, the ship is neither making way forward or going astern, and virtually stops still in the water. This manoeuvre was commonly used in these situations:

1. To communicate with another ship.

2. When lowering out or taking in the ship's boats, when receiving boats from other ships in the squadron.

3. When taking on a pilot.

4. When retrieving a man who has gone overboard.

5. When taking soundings with the lead.

6. When holding the ship to avoid going too close to the land or driving on a lee shore.

7. To hold the ship steady alongside an enemy vessel when firing a broadside.

## Reefing sails

The purpose of reefing sails is to temporarily reduce the surface area of a sail in proportion to the increase in wind velocity, rather than resort to the alternative of taking in the entire sail. The facility to reef is provided by bands of plaited rope reef points set on canvas bands sewn on both faces of the sail parallel to the upper edge of the sail. The reef points are double the diameter of the yard to which the sail is bent. Reef cringles (rope eyes) are fastened at the end of each band at the luff (vertical edge) of the sail. These cringles provide a lifting point from which to hitch up the sail using the reef tackle suspended from the yard arm when taking in a reef.

When reefing, the sail is gathered up on to the top of the yard and secured with both set of reef points, the two being temporarily tied over the top of the yard with a reef knot which can be quickly undone when taking out a reef. The number of reef bands varies according to the type of sail. The courses (foresail and mainsail) have two reef bands, whereas the fore and main topsails, which have the greatest area, have four reef bands. The mizzen topsail, being smaller, has three and the spritsail has two set in the diagonal. The quadrilateral mizzen sail has three bands parallel to the boom and the lower and topsail stunsails have one. In all cases, stunsail booms were triced (pulled) up out of the way to give the topmen room to work on the yards in safety and without hindrance to their task. The order was given as 'trice up and lay out'. Various records show that a ship with experienced topmen could reef topsails in one and a half minutes.

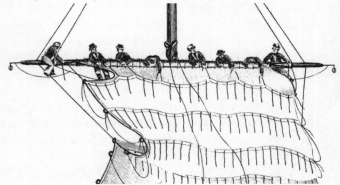

*Reefing a topsail to shorten the sail as wind pressure increases (from Darcy Lever): (a) reef tackle (b) bunt lines cased to split the wind (c) weather side caring hauled out by man (d) to spill wind. Men on yard haul sail over to man (d) using reefing points and tie reef points over yard using reef knots.*

## Reefing procedure

1. Order 'all hands reef topsails' as the topmen to go aloft into tops and crosstrees.

2. Men on deck let go the topgallant sheets and haul in the topgallant clewlines and clew up the topgallant sail to the mast head or ease the topgallant yard tye halliards and topgallant yard lifts and lower the topgallant yard.

3. Men on deck next ease the topsail yard tye halliards and topsail yard lifts and lower the topsail yard and at same time haul in on the weather (windward) braces to spill the wind from the sail.

4. Men on deck haul in on the topsail reef tackles and man the stunsail boom tricing lines at the bitts.

5. Order 'trice up and lay out'. Tricing lines are hauled up, raising the inner end of the stunsail booms canting them up at an angle and giving room for the topmen to lay out.

6. The first captain of the foretop goes to the weather yard arm and sits astride the yard, the second captain goes to the leeward yard arm.

7. First captain hauls out the weather earring of the sail and passes it to the man near him to reeve the earring through the reef cringle from aft to forward and pass it back to the first captain.

8. When the first captain the orders 'haul out to windward' the rest of the topmen manning the yard reach down and take hold of the reef points and all facing to leeward pull the sail to the weather side to allow the earring to be passed.

9. The first captain takes turns and secures the earring.

10. The first captain then orders 'haul out to leeward'. All topmen manning the yard reach down and take hold of the reef points and all facing to windward pull the sail to the lee side to allow the lee earring to be passed and secured in the same manner by the second captain.

11. All topmen manning the yard reach down and haul the sail on to the yard and make fast the reef points using reef knots.

## Safety and training

Working aloft in all weathers laid out along the yards, reefing or stowing sails, was highly precarious. Despite the dangers topmen faced on a daily basis, the annual loss of life averaged just one man per ship. Although most men were already capable of working aloft before entering into naval ships, those not adept were introduced by first practising on a spare yard, complete with footropes, longitudinally suspended above the waist of the ship, attain confidence before working out on the lower yards.

# 9

# SHIP'S BOATS AND BOAT WORK

## THE SHIP'S BOATS

The ship's boats were an essential part of the *Victory's* equipment. They were employed for a variety of reasons but were not carried as lifeboats. The boatswain's expense book for 1805 recorded that the *Victory* carried six boats:

### 34-foot launch

A large, general working boat strongly built in carvel fashion, used for conveying stores, provisions, guns, gunpowder, personnel and Marines. If required this boat could be armed with the 18-pounder carronade (see Chapter 12) mounted in her bow to provide firepower for supporting amphibious operations. The launch was also furnished with a windless used to carry and lay stream or kedge anchors. The launch could also carry guns slung underneath when landing ordnance for land use. Normally propelled by up to 16 oars doubled-banked (eight oars single-banked), it also had a mast and set of sails using lug or lateen rig.

### 32-foot barge

Clinker-built (lapstrake), this was used for conveying the admiral, high-ranking officers and dignitaries ashore or to other ships in the squadron. If necessary it would be used for amphibious landings. It was propelled by up to 12 oars doubled-banked or six oars single-banked.

### 28-foot pinnace

This clinker-built boat was mainly used for conveying the officers and other personnel ashore or to other ships in the squadron. Being relatively large, the boat could also be used for amphibious operations. It was propelled by up to eight oars doubled-banked or four oars single-banked.

### 25-foot cutter

Clinker-built and carried as a sea boat (ready for launch) – this was a general working boat for carrying stores and provisions, conveying officers and other personnel ashore to other ships in the squadron. It was propelled by up to 10 oars doubled-banked or five oars single-banked.

## 25-foot yawl

Clinker-built and carried as a sea boat (ready for launch), this served the same function as the 25-foot cutter. Both the cutter and the yawl could be rigged with a mast and lug or lateen sail.

## 18-foot cutter

A small clinker-built sea boat, mainly used for conveying officers and their baggage and other personnel ashore to other ships in the squadron. This was an ideal boat for transferring dispatches between ships.

## Boat colours

We know the colours that the *Victory's* boats were painted from the expenses entered by the carpenter '*Between 1ˢᵗ and 21ˢᵗ September*', which reads: '*To Painting the Barge, launch three yauls and a pinnace*'. The quantities and paint colours listed in the margin of this record are given in the following table:

| Item | Quantity |
|---|---:|
| Paint White | 66lb (29.7 kg) |
| Paint Black | 13lb (5.85kg) |
| Paint Yellow | 78lb (35.1kg) |
| Paint Verdegrease [sic] | 5lb (2.25kg) |
| Paint Prussian Blue | 1lb (0.45kg) |
| Oil | 8 gallons (36.36 litres) |
| Brushes | 6 |

With the exception of the 32-foot barge, all of the *Victory's* boats were painted with bland colours simply for utility needs: yellow ochre was applied internally excluding the thwarts (transverse seats), the external hull and transoms were painted with white lead. The plank sheer, rubbing strakes and uppermost plank were black, the wash strakes yellow ochre. Unlike the other boats, the Admiral's barge was prestigiously painted in olive green internally and along the plank sheer and rubbing strakes, the latter trimmed with mock gold. The external hull, transom and wash strakes were painted with white lead.

## Stowage

Most of the larger boats were stored in a fore and aft direction on the transverse skid beams in the ship's waist. In general, the cutter and yawl were either stowed slung in their quarter davits ready for launch or alternatively towed astern pending sea state.

# EMBARKING AND LAUNCHING THE SHIP'S BOATS

Getting boats in or out from the ship's waist was a complex procedure involving using the main and fore course (lower) yards as derricks (cranes) and use of the main stay. Unless circumstances dictated otherwise, it was preferable to bring the boat alongside the leeward side of the ship to avoid potential damage to the boat against the ship's hull by violent wave motion. The procedure used for embarking a boat was as follows:

1. Releasing and lowering the yard tackles suspended from the fore and main yards. This was hooked into the two lifting ring bolts within the boat; the yard tackle on the opposite side of the ship was likewise lowered and hooked on to the chains at the ship's side to in order to: (i) counteract the weight imposed on the opposing end of the respective yard; and (ii) keep the respective yards horizontal.

2. Using the yard lift, the boat was next hoisted the vertically; the fall (hauling part) of the yard tackle being taken round the jeer capstan to assist in hoisting.

3. Next, fore and main yard braces were manned in order to brace round the respective yards to 'sway' (swing) the boat inboard into the ship over the ship's waist.

4. Tackle rigged to the main stay were next lowered and then hooked into the ringbolts in the boat.

5. The weight of the boat was then transferred from the fore and main yards to the main stay by hauling in on the stay tackle and releasing the yard tackle.

6. When the weight had been fully transferred on to the main stay the yard tackle was unhooked from the boat and hoisted out of the way up to the yard arm; the opposite yard tackle was released from the chains and hoisted clear.

7. Using the stay tackle the boat was then lowered and swayed to manoeuvre her down on to its respective stowage chocks on the skid beams crossing the ship's waist.

For swaying out and lowering a boat the reverse procedure was adopted.

## Using the quarter davits

Launching the sea boats was far simpler using the quarter davits. These are pairs of hinged wooden derricks fitted to the ship's side, level with the poop deck. First, the davit topping lift tackle, which was hooked to eyebolts fastened to the poop deck and stropped under the mizzen mast top, was eased, lowering the davits to a horizontal position. Next, the davit fall tackles rigged to the outer ends of the davits were manned, and the cutter (or yawl) slowly lowered by manpower to the water. Once the bow and stern painters had been made fast, the davit tackles were unhooked from the lifting ring bolts in the boat and, with the cutter's rudder tiller pushed out away from the ship's stern, the painter was cast off, allowing the boat to veer away from the ship, the bow painter being released. For hoisting the boat back into the davits the process was reversed.

## THE SHIP'S BOATS IN BATTLE

There is a misconception that boats were lowered and filled with wardroom furniture and towed astern or cast loose before battle. While this possibly happened in the early seventeenth century, it was totally impractical and far too time-consuming to meet the aggressive demands of eighteenth-century naval warfare and the battle of Trafalgar. The *Victory* 's larger boats remained stowed in the waist during the Battle of Trafalgar and were subjected to shot damage. Two ready-use 'sea boats' were towed astern for conveying officers, receiving surrender and picking up men lost overboard (friend or foe). In the face of danger, boats from British ships at Trafalgar rescued survivors from the French *L'Achille* while she was engulfed in flames before she blew up at the end of the battle. Besides saving the French woman sailor Jeanette, one boat from HMS *Conqueror* picking men from the water actually rowed back to rescue a very distraught cat sat on the muzzle of *L'Achille's* lower guns.

# 10

# ANCHORS AWEIGH

## GROUND TACKLE

All gear related to the anchors is known as ground tackle due to its purpose of holding the ship stationary on the seabed. The *Victory* had seven anchors:

| No | Type | Weight | | | | |
|---|---|---|---|---|---|---|
| | | tons | cwt | qtr | lb | tonnes |
| 1 | Best bower anchor | 4 | 9 | 1 | 14 | 4.54 |
| 1 | Bower anchor | 4 | 8 | 2 | 22 | 4.51 |
| 2 | Sheet anchors | 4 | 4 | 3 | 12 | 4.31 |
| 1 | Stream anchor | 1 | 1 | 3 | 7 | 1.10 |
| 1 | Large kedge anchor | | 10 | 0 | 7 | 0.51 |
| 1 | Small kedge anchor | | 5 | 3 | 7 | 0.30 |

### Anchors and their uses

**Best bower anchor** This served as one of the two main anchors and was used for holding the ship in deep water. Being the heaviest and strongest anchor, it was always rigged to the starboard side of the ship.

**Bower anchor** Secured on the larboard (port) side, this served the same purpose as the best bower anchor, though it was not as strong.

**Sheet anchors** There was a sheet anchor on each side of the ship. They served as spares for the two bower anchors, should their cables part in heavy weather or the anchors become lost.

**Stream anchor** This was a lightweight anchor used for anchoring in low tide streams and shallow waters and could also be used for warping the ship. It was normally stored lashed to the starboard sheet anchor.

**Kedge anchor** These were used to keep a ship steady and clear of her bower anchor when riding in harbour. They were also used to 'kedge' or warp the ship. Kedging or warping means to haul the ship along by bringing in her cable. The kedge anchor was then taken by boat and relaid, and the operation of hauling

was repeated. This was generally done in confined waters or when there was no wind.

## Anchor stowage

Both the bower anchors were stowed hanging from catheads that protruded from the ship's side at the foremost corners of the forecastle. Fitted with pulley shivers, these stout beams acted like a crane or fixed davit with their flukes and palms resting on a block fitted to the ship's side. Although not fitted to the ship today, this block should be integral with a billboard and protective planking. The sheet anchors were stowed with their stock secured to the after end of the fore channel, their flukes and palms resting on a block fitted to the fore and aft gangways. The stream anchor was lashed to the starboard sheet anchor. The larger kedge anchor was normally stowed in the hold; the smaller kedge was stowed on the larboard (port side) mizzen channel for immediate use.

## Cables

Made of hemp and laid up (twisted) in cable form, the *Victory* carried a total of 14 individual heavy-duty cables.

| Circumference | | Diameter | | Length | | No. | Anchor type attached |
|---|---|---|---|---|---|---|---|
| in | cm | in | cm | fathoms | metres | | |
| 24 | 60.96 | 7 ¾ | 19.7 | 100 | 600 | 6 | Both bowers |
| 23 | 58.42 | 7 ¼ | 18.4 | 100 | 600 | 1 | Sheet anchors or for towing ships |
| 16 | 40.64 | 5 | 12.7 | 100 | 600 | 1 | Stream anchor or towing |
| 9 | 22.86 | 2⅞ | 7.3 | 100 | 600 | 4 | Stream anchor or towing |
| 7 ½ | 19.05 | 2⅜ | 6.0 | 100 | 600 | 1 | Large kedge anchor |
| 7 | 17.78 | 2 ¼ | 5.7 | 100 | 600 | 1 | Small kedge anchor |

## Hawsers

Made of hemp, these were laid up (twisted) in standard three-stranded rope form. The *Victory* carried a total of two hawsers that were classified as messengers or vyols and used in the process of hauling the anchor cables that were too great in diameter to pass around the capstans. They were made to length as required and were 16 inches and 14 inches in circumference (40.6cm and 35.6 cm) with a diameter of 5 inches and 4½ inches (12.7cm and 11.4cm).

## Cable stowage

Cables were generally stowed in the cable tiers either side of the orlop. Those designated for the larboard bower and sheet anchors were in the starboard tier, cables for the starboard anchors in the larboard tier. One messenger was turned up on the main capstan and laid along the gun deck ready for use; the other coiled in the hold.

## Capstans

The name capstan comes from the Latin word '*capistrum*' and the Anglo-Saxon word 'capster' meaning 'halter'. *Victory* has two capstans, the main capstan and the jeer capstan. The main capstan was used for hauling in the great anchor cable by means of a smaller continuous hawser called a messenger that was temporarily 'married' to the anchor cable by use of temporary rope lashings called nippers. This capstan comprised two main parts, sharing a common spindle extending vertically between the lower and middle gun decks. The upper part, called the drumhead, was pierced to receive 14 capstan bars, the lower part, called the trundlehead, was pierced for 12 capstan bars. With 10 men manning at each bar, the entire capstan could be operated using 260 men.

Fitted at the base of this capstan is a circular pawlhead furnished with rotating iron pawls that engaged with the iron pawl ring set into the deck planking. This integrally provided the capstan with its ratchet mechanism, which could be simply be reversed by rotating the pawls. The wooden pillars supporting the deck beams in the vicinity of this capstan were totally removed before operation. They were dislodged by means of a beam jack. Ladders and guns in close proximity were also removed to provide a clear sweep for the capstan bars.

**Jeer capstan** Virtually identical in construction to the main capstan, this was generally employed for raising masts and yards, hoisting boats, guns and stores. It could also be used for heaving anchor cables when anchoring astern. The jeer capstan fitted in the *Victory* today is the only surviving example of a late eighteenth-century capstan; and it can still be turned in its original bearings.

## WEIGHING ANCHOR AND GETTING UNDER WAY

The *Victory* and ships like her had no mechanical means of propulsion to assist ship movement when weighing anchor or anchoring. It is often wrongly believed that weighing anchor to release a ship involved the strenuous task of turning the capstan to haul the ship along on its cable to the anchor before its release from the seabed. Such extreme physical exertions were undertaken only in adverse situations. To weigh anchor, the sails were set and the ship, driven by wind power, was steered towards the point where the anchor was laid, its position marked by an anchor buoy. As the ship moved towards the anchor, the capstan was used to haul in the cable as it became slack, with some 60 men coiling the incoming cable down in the cable tier. The forward momentum of the ship would hopefully snatch the anchor from the seabed, aided by an extra strong pull on the capstan. Once the anchor was 'up and down', it was hauled 'a hawse' from where the anchor was 'fished', hoisted and 'catted' to its cathead, the ship making more sail and getting under way to clear the anchorage.

## ANCHORING

When preparing to anchor, the cable in the tier was hauled up by hand and laid out in long hanks along the lower gun deck. Having taken soundings with a leadline to confirm a sound anchorage point the *Victory* would 'heave to' (stop in the water) and drop the anchor, having a buoy attached to mark its position. Next, the topsails would be set 'aback', using the wind to drive the ship 'sternboard' (going astern) and in doing so the anchor cable was automatically paid out as through the hawse hole as the ship slowly drifted astern.

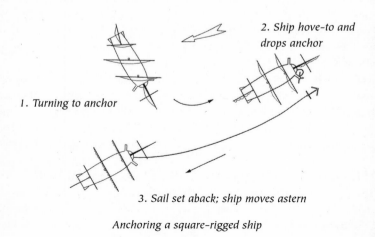

1. *Turning to anchor*

2. *Ship hove-to and drops anchor*

3. *Sail set aback; ship moves astern*

*Anchoring a square-rigged ship*

The length of cable run out was always three times the depth of the water; it is the weight of the cable that holds the ship. The anchor itself only holds the cable. Once the ship 'came up on its cable', the anchor 'tripped' by virtue of its stock and drove itself into the seabed.

The cable was turned up around the stout-built riding bitts on the lower gun deck and secured with cable stoppers, with the bitts taking the 'riding' strain of ship movement. If anchoring astern, cables were passed out through the stern ports of the lower gun deck and attached to the respective sheet or stream anchor, with cable stoppers being rigged to take the strain. Alternatively, the cable could be secured on the other set of riding bitts.

## Mooring

This method was not often used, but involved unbending (untying) the anchor cable from its anchor and securing it to the ring of a barrel-shaped wooden mooring buoy. A second mooring could be made by passing a cable astern out through the stern ports of the lower gun deck and securing it to the buoy. In either case, the riding bitts or cable stoppers were employed.

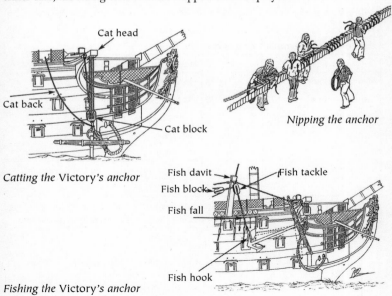

*Nipping the anchor*

*Catting the* Victory's *anchor*

*Fishing the* Victory's *anchor*

# VICTORY'S ORDNANCE

## IN ACTIVE SERVICE

During her active service, the *Victory's* ordnance armament varied according to her deployment and use. When first commissioned in 1778, she carried heavy 'brass' 42-pounders for her lower deck battery, but these were temporarily replaced by lighter iron 32-pounders, the 42-pounders being re-embarked into the ship in 1779 after which with several changes were authorised until they were recommissioned again in 1803. After refitting in 1806/07, her middle deck battery of 24-pounders was replaced with lighter 18-pounders.

### At Trafalgar

According to the gunner's records, when the *Victory* fought at the battle of Trafalgar on 21 October 1805, her ordnance totalled 105 guns, as follows:

| Deck on which mounted | No of guns | Gun type |
|---|---|---|
| Lower gun deck | 30 | Short 32-pounder carriage guns |
| Middle gun deck | 28 | Medium 24-pounder carriage guns |
| Upper gun deck | 30 | Long 12-pounder carriage guns |
| Quarter deck | 12 | Short 12-pounder carriage guns |
| Forecastle | 2 | Medium 12-pounder carriage guns |
| | 2 | 68-pounder carronades on slide carriages |
| Stored in the hold | 1 | 18-pounder carronade on a slide carriage |
| Total | 105 | |

Note: The single 18-pounder carronade on a slide carriage was reserved for mounting in the ship's launch should a boat attack be called upon or for amphibious operations.

# Technical data

| Carriage gun specifications: 42-, 32- and 24-pounders | | | |
|---|---|---|---|
| Item | Short 42-pounder (1778) | Short 32-pounder | Medium 24-pounder |
| Length of piece | 9ft 6in | 9ft 6in | 9ft 6in |
| Calibre | 16.244 | 17.725 | 19.574 |
| Weight of gun | 7,280lb | 6,160lb | 5,545lb |
| Weight of carriage | 1,456lb | 1,176lb | 1,065lb |
| Total weight of piece and carriage | 8,736lb | 7,336 lb | 6,610lb |
| Weight of shot | 42lb | 32lb | 24lb |
| Shot diameter | 6.6 in | 6.10in | 5.54in |
| Bore diameter | 6.90in | 6.35in | 5.74in |
| Powder charge standard weight | 14lb | 10.66lb | 8lb |
| Range maximum @ 6 degrees | 2740yd | 2640yd | 1980yd |
| Range point blank (gun level) | 400yd | 400yd | 400yd |
| No. of gun's crew – firing on one broadside of ship only | 16 | 14 | 12 |
| No. of gun's crew – firing both broadsides of ship simultaneously | 8 | 7 | 6 |
| Total forces exerted upon breeching rope and ship's side when fired | 18 tons | 16 tons | 18 tons |

| Carriage gun specifications: 12-pounders | | | |
|---|---|---|---|
| | Long 12-pounder | Medium 12-pounder | Short 12-pounder |
| Length of piece | 9ft 0in | 8ft 6in | 7ft 6in |
| Calibre | 23.361 | 22.063 | 19.468 |
| Weight of gun | 3,584lb | 3,528lb | 3,276lb |
| Weight of carriage | 717lb | 706lb | 628lb |
| Total weight of piece and carriage | 4,284lb | 4,234lb | 3,904lb |
| Weight of shot | 12lb | 12 lb | 12lb |
| Shot diameter | 4.40in | 4.40 in | 4.40in |
| Bore diameter | 4.64in | 4.64 in | 4.64in |
| Powder charge standard weight | 4lb | 4lb | 4lb |
| Range maximum @ 6 degrees | 1,320yd | 1,320yd | 1,320yd |
| Range point blank (gun level) | 400yd | 375yd | 375yd |
| No. of gun's crew – firing on one broadside of ship only | 10 | 10 | 10 |
| No. of gun's crew –firing both broadsides of ship simultaneously | 5 | 5 | 5 |
| Total forces exerted upon breeching rope and ship's side when fired | 10 tons | 10 tons | 10 tons |

## Carronades

Manufactured at the Carron Iron Works in Falkirk, Scotland, these short-barrelled short-range lightweight guns delivered a proportionally heavier shot with a low muzzle velocity. Highly powerful and capable of considerable damage, they were nicknamed 'smashers'. When loaded with grape shot or canister shot containing musket balls they proved an effective anti-personnel weapon. In her time the *Victory* carried carronades of various calibres mounted on the poop deck and forecastle and an 18-pounder used in her launch for amphibious attack. Specifications for carronades carried were:

| Item | 68-pounder | 12-pounder |
|---|---|---|
| Length of piece | 5ft 2in | 2ft 4in |
| Calibre | 7.70in | 5.45in |
| Weight of gun | 4,302lb | 949lb |
| Weight of round shot | 68lb | 18lb |
| Shot diameter | 7.5in | 5.04in |
| Standard powder charge weight @ 1/12 | 5.5lb | 1.5lb |
| Lowest powder charge weight @ 1/16 | 4.25lb | 1.125lb |
| Highest powder charge weight @ 1/8 | 8.5lb | 2.25lb |
| Range maximum @ 5 degrees using 1/12 charge | 1,280yd | 1,000yd |
| Range point blank (gun level) using 1/12 charge | 450yd | 270yd |
| No. of gun's crew | 6 | 5 |

## MANUFACTURING AND MATERIALS

Manufactured in cast iron, all of the standard guns in the *Victory* were of the Blomefield pattern introduced in 1787 to supersede the Armstrong pattern which, often bursting at the breech, proved a failure during the War of American Independence. Not only did bursting guns cause unnecessary fatalities to gun's crews, gunners became reluctant to fire these guns with a full charge. Blomefield guns were designed with more metal to reinforce the breech and were less likely to burst. This modification gave the British gunners greater confidence when firing their ordnance and consequently they attained superiority in gunnery throughout the French Revolutionary and Napoleonic wars. Following advances in gun manufacturing technology, the vent and the bore of the Blomefield guns were bored out after casting, a process that produced more accurate guns.

## Gun carriages

All standard long guns were mounted on wooden carriages, with the materials fastened together with wrought iron forelock and clench bolts. Carriage specifications were designed proportionally to the length of the gun, with the specific intention to transfer the recoil forces from the centre of the gun at its trunnion directly down to the hind trucks, maintaining stability as the gun came back on its breeching rope. The resultant forces were then transferred to the ship's side as the gun halted its maximum recoil. The breeching rope was of a length designed to minimise the distance needed to run the gun forward into its firing position. Because 24- and 32-pounder guns recoiled with far greater force, these were rigged with additional preventer breeching ropes.

| Gun carriage components and materials | |
| --- | --- |
| **Components** | **Material** |
| Cheek x 2 | Elm |
| Transom | Elm |
| Fore axletree | Oak |
| Hind axletree | Oak |
| Fore truck | Elm |
| Hind truck | Elm |
| Stool bed | Oak |
| Quoin | Oak |

## Side arms and gunnery equipment

Each gun was to be furnished with their tools known as 'side arms':

1. Rammer – to ram home shot, charge and wads.
2. Sponge – to swab out the gun with water to extinguish smouldering debris.
3. Wad hook (or worm) – to remove wads and burning debris.
4. Combined rammer and sponge.
5. Combined flexible rope rammer and sponge – used when loading or swabbing with the gun when port lids are deliberately temporarily shut.
6. Handspikes (or crows) made of ash – to manoeuvre the gun carriage sideways when pointing or traversing the gun.
7. Ladle – used for inserting a cartridge.

8. Cartridge pricker – thin brass-pointed skewer 10in long.

9. Vent reamer – steel or brass twisted skewer to clear vent of carbon deposits.

**Other necessary equipment included:**

1. Wooden swab bucket.

2. Wooden sand scuttle.

3. Wooden match tub (there were two types: open top or closed top).

4. Slow match: short lengths of specially manufactured rope soaked in potassium nitrate ($KNO_3$) that burned at two feet per hour.

5. Wooden linstock to hold the slow match.

6. Wooden 'salt box' to contain ready use charges (lidded powder box with leather hinges and brass fittings).

7. Iron crows – crowbars used as handspikes.

8. Gunlock – spring-operated device that mechanically strikes a flint to produce an ignition spark.

9. Firing tubes – preformed goose quills filled with very fine gunpowder mixed with spirits of wine.

10. 'Cases of wood' – cylindrical lidded containers for conveying cartridges from magazines to replenish the 'salt boxes (see page 98).

## Powder magazines

The *Victory* had three powder magazines: the grand magazine and two ready hanging magazines. The former, approximately 32 square feet in area and 10 feet high, consisted of three main compartments creating an industrial assembly line. First was the pallating flat, containing 35 tons of gunpowder in 784 barrels, each containing 100lb (45kg) of powder. If ignited, this amount of gunpowder had the explosive equivalent of 47 tons of TNT. This had a specially constructed pallated deck to deter moisture from below. All bulkheads forming this room are lined with copper to deter sparks or lined with fireproof plaster and mortar.

Next was the filling room, where cartridges were made up from gunpowder poured from the casks into a large oak bin. This room was furnished on each side with cartridge racks for the 32-pounder guns. All divisional bulkheads were lined with copper and the deck lined with lead. In the centre was an integrally built light room specially constructed to contain large lanthorns doubly shielded within light boxes behind glazed sashes with copper grills and wooden shutters. For safety the lanthorns could only be lit from a segregated light room entered beyond the magazine. All cartridge filling was supervised by the Yeoman of the Powder Room. This room was also used for making signal rockets and charging hand grenades. In the wings either side of the magazine powder and filling rooms were the barrel rooms for storing used 'shaken down' powder casks for return to the Ordnance Board. Because gunpowder barrel staves were coated with residue and a fire hazard, these compartments were lined with slit deals (timber), plaster and mortar.

The two 'hanging 'magazines' located on the orlop containing ready to use cartridges were effectively box rooms suspended between the orlop and the hold. Access to each was via a single door, with a second door into an enclosed segregated light room. Internally furnished with cartridge racks, the decks and bulkheads were lined with copper. The foremost hanging magazine supplied cartridges for the 24-pounder guns. The aftermost magazine, relative to suitable ascending ladders, provided cartridges for the 12-pounder guns on the upper gun deck and quarterdeck.

## Shot stowage

The *Victory* carried 120 tons of solid iron round shot: 80 tons within two shot lockers in the hold and a further 40 tons below the coalhole. At the Battle of Trafalgar, which lasted about five hours, the *Victory* expended 2669 round shot weighing a total of 27 tons. Bar, chain and elongating shot of various calibres was also carried. Ready-use shot was stowed in racks surrounding hatchways. In battle, shot was hoisted to each deck in baskets or nets using whips (a single block through which a rope was passed).

## Ammunition supply

In battle, shot was hoisted to each deck in baskets using whips. Gunpowder cartridges were transferred from the magazines to the gun decks within cylindrical 'cases of wood'. These were passed by hand by a train of people up though hatchways on predetermined routes, with boys or runners filling the salt boxes behind the guns. For efficiency in supply and demand, the *Victory* needed 80–100 people undertaking this task; those involved were stewards and the like, non-combatants and women.

# 12

# TRAINING THE GREAT GUNS

## GUN DRILL

Regarding training the gun's crews, the gunner *'is to see that they perform every part of the exercise with the utmost correctness, particularly explaining to them, and the strongly reinforcing, the necessity of pointing their guns carefully before firing them, and spunging* [sic] *them well, with the touch hole close stopped immediately after they have been fired.'*

## Training procedure

The following procedure relates to gunnery training and does not reflect the more rapid practical procedure undertaken in the heat of battle.

| | **Words of command** | **Observation or action taken** |
|---|---|---|
| | **The authorised gun drill to exercise the great guns** | |
| 1 | Take heed | To get the attention of the people |
| 2 | Silence | To prevent the people talking |
| 3 | Cast loose your guns | Cast off side tackles, breeching ropes and muzzle lashings |
| 4 | Seize the breechings | Ensure ends of breeching rope well secured to the ship's side ringbolts |
| 5 | Take out the tampion | Remove stopper from muzzle of gun |
| 6 | Take off the apron | Remove lead apron protecting vent of the gun |
| 7 | Unstop the touch hole | Remove wax plug from vent |
| 8 | Handle the pricking wire | Take the cartridge pricker ready in hand |
| 9 | Prick the cartridge | Firmly pierce cartridge by inserting cartridge pricker |
| 10 | Handle the powder horn | Take powder horn ready in hand |
| 11 | Prime | Pour powder from powder horn into the pan and vent |
| 12 | Bruise the priming | Firm down powder with knuckle to prevent it blowing away |

| 13 | Secure the powder horn | Keep powder horn away from gun |
|----|------------------------|-------------------------------|
| 14 | Take hold of the apron | Take apron ready in hand |
| 15 | Cover the vent | Replace apron over vent to prevent inadvertent firing |
| 16 | Handle your crows and handspikes | Take up crows and handspikes ready in hand |
| 17 | Point the gun to the object | Using crows and handspikes move gun carriage |
| 18 | Lay down your crows and handspikes | Lay crows and handspikes down on deck out of way |
| 19 | Take off the apron | Remove lead apron. |
| 20 | Take your match and blow it | Take slow match ready in hand on its linstock from match tub well behind the gun |
| 21 | Fire | Shout 'make ready' and touch off the powder in the pan and stand clear. |
| 22 | Stop the touch hole | Stop the vent with your thumb (see page 102) |
| 23 | Handle the spunge staff | Take spunge staff ready in hand |
| 24 | Sponge the gun | Insert sponge into the bore of gun (see page 102) |

| **The reloading drill** | | |
|----|------------------------|-------------------------------|
| 25 | Handle the cartridge | Pass cartridge from salt box to loader at muzzle of gun (see page 102) |
| 26 | Put it into the gun | See important instructions on page 102 |
| 27 | Wad your cartridge | The load wad helps compression and bed for round shot |
| 28 | Handle the rammer | Take rammer ready in hand |
| 29 | Ram home wad and cartridge | Using rammer drive in cartridge and wad shot hard up against the bottom of the bore of the gun |
| 30 | Unstop the touch hole | Stop thumbing the vent |
| 31 | Handle the pricking wire | Take cartridge pricker ready in hand |
| 32 | Try if the cartridge be home | Using pricker feel if the cartridge is well in the end of the bore |
| 33 | Draw the rammer | So that the cartridge is proved well home, withdraw rammer completely from gun |
| 34 | Shot the gun | Load round shot |

| 35 | Wad | Load a second wad to prevent the round shot rolling out |
| 36 | Ram home wad and shot | Using rammer drive in wad and shot hard up against the cartridge |
| 37 | Draw the rammer | Withdraw the rammer completely from gun |
| 38 | Stop the touch hole | Stop the vent with thumb |
| 39 | Lay on the apron | Replace apron over vent to prevent inadvertent firing |
| 40 | Run out the gun | Take up side tackles and haul gun out through gun port |

| The authorised gun drill in battle assuming the gun has already been fired | | |
|---|---|---|
| | **Words of command** | **Observation or action taken** |
| 1 | Stop the touch hole | Serve the vent with your thumb |
| 2 | Search the gun | Using wadhook, clear out any debris (every four rounds) |
| 3 | Sponge the gun | Insert wetted sponge down into bore of gun. |
| 4 | Load with cartridge | Pass cartridge from salt box to loader at muzzle of gun |
| 5 | Load with wad | Load wad to provide bed for round shot |
| 6 | Ram home wad and cartridge | Ram home both to compress the charge |
| 7 | Prick the cartridge | Pierce the cartridge |
| 8 | Shot the gun | Load round shot |
| 9 | Wad the shot | Load and ram second wad to prevent shot rolling out |
| 10 | Draw the rammer | Withdraw the rammer completely from gun |
| 11 | Stop the touch hole | Stop the vent with thumb |
| 12 | Run out the gun | Take up side tackles and run out the gun through gun port |
| 13 | Point the gun | Move gun carriage as required using crows and handspikes |
| 14 | Unstop the touch hole | Stop thumbing the vent |
| 15 | Prime the gun | Prime the pan and bruise the priming |
| 16 | Make ready | Take slow match in hand on its linstock from match tub and blow it – gun's crew, stand clear |
| 17 | Fire | Touch off the powder in the pan and stand clear |

Important instructions: The stop hole, or vent, is to be closed using the thumb every time any item is passed into the gun muzzle. This safety procedure is carried out to:

1. Prevent hot embers or debris from being forced up through the vent and inadvertently igniting loose powder external to the gun.

2. Prevent hot embers or debris from being drawn down through the vent into the bore of the gun where they could inadvertently ignite the charge as it is loaded.

If firing the gun using a flint-operated gunlock the same gun drill procedures applied. A linstock and slow match in a match tub was to be kept close at hand for instant readiness should the mechanical gunlock fail.

## Crew numbers on each gun

| Number of gun's crew per gun | | |
|---|---|---|
| Size of gun | Total crew | If firing both broadsides |
| 42-pounder | 16 | 8 |
| 32-pounder | 14 | 7 |
| 24-pounder | 12 | 6 |
| 12-pounder | 10 | 5 |
| 9-pounder | 8 | 4 |
| 6-pounder | 6 | 3 |
| 4-pounder | 4 | 2 |
| 3-pounder | 4 | 2 |

The number of men dedicated to each gun's crew was determined by the weight and type of gun. The calculation used to determine the number of men required to operate a standard carriage gun was as follows.

$$\frac{\text{Weight of the actual gun (lb) + Weight of gun carriage (lb)}}{500\text{lb}}$$

The division figure of 500lb was the estimated maximum weight a single man could haul.

The number of crew needed for the carronades was between four and six,

depending on the weight of shot being fired.

If firing broadsides on both sides of the ship simultaneously, gun's crew numbers were either halved or the gun's crews moved to the next adjacent gun to sponge out and reload. Firing was left to a single captain of the gun as necessary.

## Frequency of gun drill

Gun drills were carried out as often as possible depending on operational ability. Gun drills using live ammunition were limited to once weekly to conserve shot and gunpowder. Live firing was not undertaken if the ship was in close proximity to the enemy to avoiding drawing attention to the position. All drills were timed by the officers governing each deck or battery. The expected sequence of firing and reloading generally took one and a half minutes, although most well trained crews managed to fire a round every minute.

## Attaining accuracy

Although broadside firing was standard in a sea fight it was often at point blank (no elevation), within musket shot range of 225–300ft (75–100m) and more often less at pistol shot range of 50–70ft (16–23m). Training often necessitated live firing 'at a mark', the object being a target set adrift, with guns crews learning to train and point (aim) their gun.

If training in oblique firing i.e. 45 degrees, guns could be slewed around accordingly using handspikes and crows, and by unhooking the side tackle from both carriage and the ship's side. One end of the tackle was then rehooked into to an eyebolt near the rear of the carriage the other end hooked into an eyebolt fitted at the ship's side between the gun ports. This was known as a quarter bolt. This method provided greater mechanical advantage. If greater elevation was needed beyond adjusting of the quoins (wedges) under the breach then the rear trucks of the carriage were removed by lifting the carriage with handspikes.

# 13

# THE BROADSIDE OF BATTLE

*'No captain can do any wrong if he lays his ship alongside that of the enemy'*
HORATIO NELSON

## THE BROADSIDE AND THE LINE OF BATTLE

The concept of broadside firing from ships formed into a line of battle into an opposing line of enemy ships was formulated during the Dutch Wars in the mid-seventeenth century. Prior to this, naval warfare followed a more fluid form of engagement with ships manoeuvring quite independently when attacking an opposing fleet, a method used by Drake and Hawkins when fighting against the Spanish Armada in 1588. This freestyle type of engagement went out of practice during the seventeenth century when Oliver Cromwell appointed 'generals at sea' into his Commonwealth Navy and naval warfare as reorganised in a military fashion with commanders of ships and squadrons compelled to operate like regiments the field. The rigid 'line of battle' thus created maximised the control and effect of gunfire into enemy ships. Controlled broadside firing in line ahead proved highly effective and affected ship design; more weakly constructed heads and sterns became vulnerable if attacked from afore or abaft.

The tactic of broadside firing prevailed as standard practice until the War of American Independence when Admiral Rodney broke away from the rigid Admiralty instructions at the Battle of the Saints against the French fleet under de Grasse on 12 April 1782. Prior to this, any officer who did not fight in the authorised line of battle 'did so at his own peril' and faced the wrath of the Admiralty. Nelson is repeatedly given considerable credit for using an unauthorised tactic of attack at the Battle of Trafalgar when he directed his ships to pass through the enemy line. Although his line of attack proved successful at this battle, this idea fortifies the Nelson 'myth'. However, this revolutionary form of naval warfare should be credited rightfully to other tacticians such as Rodney and Boscawan.

The key elements that proved British naval supremacy were good seamanship, gunnery and training. Ironically the form of fighting employed at Trafalgar, whereby ships attacked individually or jointly and subdued single ships piecemeal under consolidated broadsides, very much returned to the type of tactics used against the Spanish Armada at the end of the sixteenth century. Breaking away from the rigid line of battle also provided ship designers with greater scope to build ships with less vulnerable heads and sterns. Robert Seppings introducing the round bow (later fitted to the *Victory*) and round stern. The new round bow and stern equally enabled guns to be mounted in these parts of a ship, giving 360 degrees of defence.

The weight of iron discharged from single-shotted guns fired from one single broadside of the *Victory* was 1,148lb (522kg) or 0.65 imperial tons. If firing both larboard and starboard broadsides simultaneously the combined broadside weight of the *Victory's* firepower doubled to 2,296lb (1.25 tons of iron).

This weight was 35 per cent greater than the massed firepower of 1,704lb (0.76 tons) discharged from the 161 guns that Field Marshall Wellington had at his disposal supporting his allied army in the field at the Battle Waterloo against the French in 1815. The *Victory's* first opening broadside at Trafalgar, fired through the stern of the French flagship *La Bucenture*, was treble-shotted; the weight of broadside in this instance was 3,444lb (1,566kg) or 1.9 imperial tons.

If all guns from each of the 33 British ships present at Trafalgar (frigates and smaller vessels included) fired one round only, the total broadside weight of iron round shot expended amounted to 51,944lb (23.21 imperial tons).

## Muzzle velocity

The larger 32-pounder Blomefield pattern guns were very powerful. Using a full charge of about 11lb (5kg) of gunpowder, i.e. 1/3 the weight of the shot, the muzzle velocity of these guns firing a single 32lb (14.4kg) shot would be between 1500 and 1600 feet per second (487 m/s). These figures equate to between 1023 and 1091 miles an hour (1646 and 1755km/hour). Therefore projectiles fired from smooth bored muzzle loading guns were supersonic, the shot taking 3.3 seconds to travel a mile.

One of the most remarkable incidents recorded about gunfire was the death of Thomas Whipple who was serving in the *Victory* as Captain Hardy's clerk at Trafalgar. Whipple actually died unmarked. This was caused by the vortex created by a round shot passing his head and the resulting vacuum sucking all of the air from his lungs. In effect, the man was instantly suffocated as he stood on the quarterdeck.

## Recoil

According to Isaac Newton's law of physics, *'for every action there is an equal and opposite reaction'*. This statement in relation to the gun or other contrivance that discharges a projectile under force, be it either round shot, rocket or even the simple arrow, is called recoil. The recoil of a naval gun is constrained by heavy breeching ropes secured to both the breech of the gun and to a pair of ringbolts firmly secured in the ship's side. The length of a breeching rope is calculated as three times the length of the barrel of the gun measured from the muzzle to the breech ring. Not only does the breeching rope maintain that the gun is secured to the ship's side, its actual length is determined such that the gun can only recoil sufficient distance to bring the muzzle about 18 inches in from the gun port, thereby providing sufficient room to swab and reload the gun. If the breeching rope was any longer, then greater physical effort and time would be wasted hauling the gun forward back to its firing position with its muzzle outside the gun port.

According to Major Adrian Caruana of the Royal Artillery who carried out experimental firing with an unrestrained 32-pounder carriage gun using a full charge of powder and a projectile, the gun and its carriage (with a total weight of 69cwt 2qtr 11lb (31.2 tonnes)), recoiled a distance of 50ft 2in (15.3m) about 3ft (91cm) greater than the breadth of the lower gun deck of a 74-gun ship. Calculations made by his colleague Major Denny Elvin determined that the gun and carriage were reversing (recoiling) at a speed of 6ft per second before the overall weight brought the gun brought it to a standstill. The forces exerted on the two ringbolts at the ship's side to which the two ends of a breeching rope were secured were quite considerable.

Calculations infer that the total weight exerted by a single 32-pounder is estimated as 8 imperial tons per ringbolt; 7 tons for a 24-pounder and 6 tons for a 12-pounder. Using these figures as a guideline, when the *Victory* fired a single-shotted broadside, the total estimated force on the hull frames on one side of the ship would be around 1300 tons. Because of this colossal strain on the fabric of the hull, the practice of firing a broadside in a ripple form from head to stern was introduced, simply to allow the hull to absorb the concerted shock if all guns fired at precisely the same time. For identical reasons, a similar concept was introduced into armies when they were marching across bridges, where they would break step to prevent the resonance of concerted foot movement weakening the structure of the bridge.

## Gunpowder and its properties

The propellant force that produced such muzzle velocities was standard gunpowder made from the following three materials:

| The constituents of gunpowder | | |
|---|---|---|
| *Chemical* | *Quantity* | *Purpose* |
| Potassium nitrate (saltpetre) | 75 per cent | Provided oxygen to increase the combustion rate |
| Charcoal (carbon) | 15 per cent | Provided fuel and heat in the form of carbon dioxide to assist the combustion process |
| Sulphur | 10 per cent | Acted as a catalyst (chemical reaction) with the charcoal in the combustion process |

The saltpetre provided extra oxygen, while all three ingredients reacted together to form nitrogen and carbon dioxide and potassium sulphide. The expanding gases (nitrogen and carbon dioxide), provided the propelling action. Rated as a highly explosive compound, gunpowder was only 35 per cent weaker in destructive power than modern trinitrotoluene (TNT). When gunpowder was ignited it expanded to 300 per cent of its own volume providing a highly effective propellant. The total broadside weight of gunpowder expended by the 33 British ships present at Trafalgar if firing one round only amounted to 16,032lb (17.7 imperial tons).

## Destructive power

At a point blank range of 370 yards (338.33m) a 32lb shot travelling at these velocities could pass through 3 feet (0.9m) of oak or 6ft (1.83m) of fir or pine. A superb example of this can be seen on the battle-damaged section of the *Victory's* original pine foremast now displayed in the ship; this was shot clean through at Trafalgar. The muzzle velocity of the smaller calibre 12- and 24-pounder guns was only marginally slower than that of the 32-pounders, although the firepower was proportionally reduced. In comparison to the long guns, the carronades, had a considerably low muzzle velocity but firing a proportionally heavier shot at low velocity these guns had the advantage of creating greater damage at short range. Rather than punching its way through timber the shot virtually 'churned its way through', making repairs to the hull far more difficult.

## Shot firing experiment

To ascertain firepower and damage effect caused by a 32lb solid iron round shot an experiment was conducted at Fort Nelson, Portsmouth, jointly orchestrated by Nick Hall, Keeper of the Royal Armouries, and the author. This involved firing 32lb solid iron shot from an original cast iron 32-pounder through oak planks 9in (22.9 cm) thick and 12in (30.48cm) broad from a range of 25 yards (22.9 metres) or 'pistol shot range', typical of the range at which most sea battles like Trafalgar were fought. The normal gunpowder charge for a 32lb shot was about 11lb (5kg) or one-third of the weight of the shot, we only used 4lb (1.8kg) for this experiment. Although this produced less kinetic energy than a full charge, the effects on the timber were remarkable. The first shot punched straight through, as expected. Although the second shot hit a knot in the timber, it still continued to pass through the plank, but the wood surrounding the knot actually sprang back and reformed due to the inherent strength of its growth around the knot. This type of damage demonstrated that repairing this kind of hole was far more difficult than stopping up a clean hole.

Although we know from historical records that flying wood splinters inflicted horrendous physical wounds on the men and certainly kept the surgeons and mates busy belowdecks, the most surprising discovery surrounding this firing experiment was that wood splinters, as a result of the kinetic energy behind the shot, firmly penetrated into nearby timber like nails. This result indicated that the same effect would have been produced inside ships during battle. Colloquially known as 'spalling', the same kind of effect is produced by fragmented metal inside military tanks when hit by shells, with the resultant shards mutilating the crew within. Experiments with explosives proved that something as light as straw can be driven into timber by kinetic forces.

## Psychological effect of firing broadsides

Despite the awesome damage, terrible carnage, casualties and injuries inflicted by a well-timed broadside, it was often the psychological effect that had the greatest impact. The practice of creating sudden impact to mentally break the human condition and will to fight has long been used in warfare, from the swift-moving chariots used as archery or javelin platforms commanded by the Egyptian king Thutmos III during his campaigns in Syria and the Euphrates Valley to the prolonged bombardment of the trenches before infantrymen 'went over the top' during the First World War. Other examples of creating *blitzkrieg* terror are the continuous bombing of London and German cities in the 1940s and the use of napalm during the Vietnam War. Such opening overtures have a devastating effect on the human mind and nervous system, creating what is commonly called 'shell shock'. It is regrettable that military and naval records from the eighteenth century do not provide statistics of men who suffered from this mental phenomenon.

## Noise of gunfire

It is recorded that the noise of gunfire at the Battle of Trafalgar which took place some 12 to 15 miles out at sea could be heard 60 miles inland in Spain; a total distance of 75 miles away. The tremendous explosive noise of a broadside was terrifying enough to break the morale of a ship's crew under fire. Although it is often believed that gunners suffered temporary or sustained deafness after a sea fight, gunfire noise is only created at the muzzle of the end of a gun. Consequently the noise heard externally was far greater than that heard on board on the gun deck. This noise of would have had a profound psychological effect upon the crew of the ship being attacked if they were not returning fire simultaneously. If they were then they would feel the same sense of release described overleaf despite the fact that each individual could be a casualty within seconds.

## Operating the guns

Operating naval guns was physically and mentally exhausting. Getting into close action quickly kept the guns crews fresh for as long as possible. The actual act of firing an opening broadside and the noise it created provided a mental release to the gun's crews delivering the broadside after the often prolonged anticipation of fighting as opposing fleets manoeuvred in preparation for battle.

A well-timed broadside could defeat an enemy ship in a very short time, with boarding and hand-to-hand combat being only the finishing process of taking possession of the ship. Not only did getting in very close alongside an enemy ship and hitting her hard have the desired effect upon an enemy, it also reduced the inevitable waste of shot and powder of ineffective long-range gunnery.

Such tactics were employed by Captain (later Admiral) Edward Hawke at Rear-Admiral William Rowley's engagement against the French-Spanish fleet off Toulon on 11 February 1744. During this action Hawke closed his 70-gun *Berwick* within half pistol shot range of the Spanish 60-gun *Poder,* and fired his opening broadside killing 27 men and dismount several of *Poder's* lower deck guns. Within 20 minutes the *Berwick's* broadsides dismasted her opponent and inflicted more than 200 casualties, compelling *Poder* to strike her colours while losses in the *Berwick* were just six men. In cases where a ship had a depleted crew caused by disease or misadventure, reduced numbers of men were sometimes divided into groups to work along one side of the deck. Commodore Anson used this method in the 60-gun *Centurion* when he attacked a Spanish treasure galleon in the Pacific. Here the crew '*used an ingenious system of fire power. Since their guns were less than half-manned down a crew of flying cannoneers ran from one gun to the other reloading and firing so that the firing into the enemy ship was continuous. Within a half-mile range the Centurion's guns were able to inflict heavy damage'.* This tactic of getting in very close to cause substantial casualties was also used by Admiral Edward Boscawen at the Battle of Lagos in 1759 and by successive admirals, including Nelson.

## Rate of fire

It was essential to deliver a fast firing rate in order to subdue an enemy ship as quickly as possible. Likewise the need to establish a faster rate of fire as than an opponent effectively reduced casualties on one's own ship. When the *Victory* fired her treble-shotted larboard broadside guns through the stern of the 80-gun French flagship *La Bucentaure* at Trafalgar, this singular volley dismounted 25 per cent of her guns and caused some 360 casualties; the shock of this devastation created all manner of confusion between decks. This was further compounded by the fact that the British warships following in the *Victory's* wake raked *La Bucentaure* in a similar manner, leaving few of her remaining crew able to stand.

At Trafalgar most British ships were firing off three broadsides to every single broadside fired by the enemy. Extensive training was given to gun's crews in order for them to fire and reload their guns rapidly. Most captains expected their gunners to complete the entire cycle of firing (swabbing worming and loading the gun with its charge, wad and shot) in 90 seconds. Records indicate that this sequence was often achieved in under a minute. This firing rate could only be maintained at the opening of battle as fatigue, injury or loss of life began to deplete the efficiency of a gun's crew.

## Manpower

The total number of gun's crew for each type of gun is given on page 102. The number given for specific gun types also includes the gun's crew that would man the gun on the opposite side of the ship. For example, a gun's crew manning in No. 6 gun lower gun deck larboard (port) also served No. 6 gun lower gun deck starboard. Although this theoretically reduced the division of manpower, the limitation was necessary as it was impractical to berth and feed so many men. If the ship were fighting on one side only then a gun would be fully manned; if the ship were fighting on both broadsides the entire gun's crew was divided between the guns on each side. Or the gun's crew would cross the deck after firing one gun to fire its opposite number. Although the physical acts of swabbing, loading and firing were reduced when employing this practice, the firing rate remained consistent. Individual members of gun's crews were also designated to undertake emergency tasks in battle; this was given on the ship's Quarter Bill. The Quarter Bill of the 74-gun *Goliath* was as follows:

| Task allocation from each gun's crew | | |
|---|---|---|
| Letter | Task or station | No. |
| B | Boarding or repelling borders | 2 |
| S | Sail trimming | 2 |
| P | Manning the pumps | 2 |
| F | Fire fighting | 1 |
| L | Holding lanthorn (night action) | 1 |

In such circumstances, each gun's crew would be reduced by the same number of people according to the emergency arising; the reduction of manpower was proportional and did not affect the overall efficiency, although the firing rate would also diminish proportionately with the men returning to their guns on completion. The firing rate would greatly diminish in a hard-pressed fight due to casualties. Under these extreme circumstances, the firing rate was controlled by individual gun captains firing when they were able and ready. A system similar to that adapted by Anson on the *Centurion* would have been used if boarders, sail trimmers and fire fighters were called away from the guns in the middle of the engagement.

# 14

# 'BOARDERS AWAY'

## WATCH AND STATION BILL

Although the ship's company was divided into a two-watch system and into gun's crews for battle stations, many unforeseen conditions were generated in battle and needed attention. To meet these demands each gun crew member was allocated an additional duty, denoted by a letter against his name on the station bill; these were B, F, L, P and S.

**B is for Boarder** Men denoted B were to leave the gun to form up boarding parties to capture enemy ships or repel boarders from enemy ships.

**F is for Fire** Men denoted F were to leave the gun to form firefighting parties using hoses or buckets or the portable fire engine.

**L is for Lanthorn** Men denoted L held the lanthorn when night firing.

**P is for Pumps** Men denoted P were to leave the gun to man the bilge pumps and hoses to remove seawater from below waterline shot damage. They also manned the elm tree pumps to pump seawater to firefighting hoses or filling fire buckets.

**S is for Sail** Men denoted S were to leave the gun to attend sail handling when manoeuvring the ship in battle.

Whatever situation arose each separate gun's crew along the decks would be marginally reduced and while this proportional manpower loss may have affected the overall gunnery firing rate, consistent effectiveness was maintained.

### Edged boarding weapons

When boarding enemy ships, officers were generally armed with pistols, sword or hanger (curved sword); the midshipmen also had their dirks, although any weapon found at hand during the ensuing mêlée was used, including wooden belaying pins. The marines had their own muskets and bayonets, and various weapons were distributed around the decks of the ship when clearing for action for immediate defensive or offensive use. They generally included broad flat-bladed cutlasses, tomahawks (a hand axe with a spike) and half pikes, the later item being a shorter version of the 14-foot long pikes used by the land armies during the seventeenth century. Seven-foot half pikes were far too unwieldy for offensive use when boarding another ship as they could snag in rigging. Used in a phalanx of men, the half pike did prove an ideal defensive weapon for repelling a horde of boarders.

### Firearms
Also distributed around the decks were the India Pattern 'Tower' flintlock muskets with bayonets. Specially adapted for sea service use, these had a barrel length of 37 inches (93.98cm) of 0.75 calibre made of tempered seamless carbon steel. Using a standard gunpowder-filled paper cartridge, they fired a ball of 0.75 inches diameter a maximum range of 50 to 75 yards.

Sea service muskets were shorter than the military equivalent, but they also had a square butt with a brass butt plate. In most cases, the metalwork was blackened to protect it in a salty environment and, for similar reasons, the ram rods were often made from wood. Also at hand were boxes of pistols primed and loaded. With a barrel length of 19 inches (48.25cm) of 0.75 calibre, these had a maximum range of 16–25 yards and were only effective between two and five yards. Not easily reloaded in the heat of battle, their brass-cupped butts proved an effective club.

### Grenades
Boxes of fixed (fused) grenades were also kept at hand for boarding. These comprised a hollow spherical iron ball filled with gunpowder and fitted with a wooden seven-second fuse.

## THE ACT OF BOARDING
When the order '*Boarder's away*' was called the men denoted as B left their guns, picked up their arms and rallied to their offensive and defensive role as directed by the officers. As a historical re-enactor I have found that the best combination of weapons for hand-to-hand cut and slash fighting is to wield a cutlass in one hand and tomahawk in the other, the cutlass directed at the body, the tomahawk at the head.

# 15

# TRAFALGAR
# (AL-TARAFAL-AL-AGHAR الطرف الأغر)

## PRELUDE

Popular history has often suggested that Nelson's victorious battle against the combined fleet of French and Spanish warships off Cape Trafalgar on 21 October 1805 completely stopped Napoleon Bonaparte from invading Britain, but this was not strictly the case and the actual facts behind the story are far more intriguing.

*Map of Cape Trafalgar*

Europe had been at war with Revolutionary France since 1793, during which time Britain encouraged a number of coalitions to counteract French expansionism. By 1801 all countries involved were financially exhausted. The resultant stalemate was politically resolved by the Treaty of Amiens, signed on 25 March 1802, closing the war of the Second Coalition, with Britain recognising the French Republic. Despite French colonial possessions being restored, the intended peace was fraught with territorial disputes arising over France's imperialist policies in the West Indies, Italy and Switzerland, added to which Britain refused to evacuate Malta as agreed. Further political turmoil ensued when Bonaparte sold Louisiana to the United States to prevent its capture by Britain. The ensuing diplomatic crisis was not helped when Britain rejected the idea of mediation by Tsar Alexander, and with Spain allying herself to France, Britain had no option but to declare war on France on 18 May 1803, starting the Napoleonic Wars that would rage throughout Europe and Russia for the next 12 years.

The frail interim peace had actually provided Bonaparte with the ideal opportunity to create a new invasion army known as the *Armée des côtes de l'Océan* (Army of the Ocean Coasts) or the *Armée de l'Angleterre* (Army of England). This potential force of 200,000 men was gathered and trained at camps at Boulogne, Bruges and Montreuil. Furthermore, hundreds of troop-carrying craft were built at great expense to the French budget.

## THE CAMPAIGN

Threatened by imminent invasion, Britain stood alone; at this time any victory was welcome. What prevented an invasion was a series of events, the first involving ingenuous political juggling by Prime Minister William Pitt (the Younger) to create a new alliance with Austria and Russia on the eastern flank of France; the Bank of England financially supporting Austria to allow this. The second lay with the Royal Navy, the Mediterranean fleet under Vice-Admiral Horatio Lord Nelson and the Channel Fleet commanded by Vice-Admiral William Cornwallis. Although operating independently, it was the consolidated operations of these two fleets and the exertions of Lord Barham, Admiral Charles Middleton, who, as First Lord of the Admiralty at Whitehall, strategically created what was later dubbed the Trafalgar campaign.

## Blockade

Bonaparte's invasion plan necessitated a large naval fleet to enter the English Channel to cover his troops crossing from France. While Nelson blockaded the Mediterranean naval ports of Toulon and Cartagena to prevent French and Spanish warships uniting and breaking out into the Atlantic and entering the western approaches of the Channel, Cornwallis diligently blockaded of the French Atlantic fleets based in Brest and Rochefort. Cornwallis also had detached squadrons watching over the Spanish warships in El Ferrol, La Coruña and Cadiz.

Historians have often underestimated the role Cornwallis played in the overall campaign. Regardless of season, weather or sea state, his ships and resources, stretched beyond capacity, Cornwallis's tenacity and maintenance of an iron grip on Britain's enemy has all too often been overshadowed by Nelson's victory at Trafalgar. It was Cornwallis' vigilant squadrons that incapacitated any attempt by Bonaparte to invade. It was through the exertions of both Nelson's and Cornwallis's fleets that Pitt was given valuable time to play his political masterstroke involving alliances with Austria and Russia.

What is often misunderstoon is that by August 1805 Bonaparte had already dissolved his great invasion plan. Now threatened on his Eastern flank Bonaparte had no choice but to order Marshal Ney, commander of the Grande Armée, to break camp at Boulogne and march his troops east before the armies of Austrian and Russia could combine. Regarding the Battle of Trafalgar, there is a misunderstanding of where Vice-Admiral Pierre-Charles Villeneuve was leading the combined Franco-Spanish fleet under his command after sailing from Cadiz. It was not heading north towards Britain to cover the invasion, it was actually sailing east into the Mediterranean to fulfil a revised role related to the new campaign against Austrian and Russian forces when it was forced into battle by Nelson.

## British and French tactical objectives

The prime objective of Nelson's Mediterranean command was to prevent the French fleet under Vice-Admiral Villeneuve breaking out of Toulon and marrying up with other French and Spanish squadrons.

The prime objective for Villeneuve, in compliance with Bonaparte's initial invasion plan, was to evade Nelson's ships and sail west to combine forces with a squadron of 21 French warships from the French Atlantic ports and attack British possessions in the Caribbean. The purpose of this was twofold:

1. To threaten British merchants by damaging the highly profitable sugar trade; the resultant financial losses incurred would hopefully destabilise Pitt's minority Tory government, allowing the Whig opposition to seize power. It was believed that the liberal-minded Whigs, led by Charles Fox, were more likely to seek a peace deal with France.

2. To draw ships from away from Cornwallis's defensive Channel fleet to protect the colonial trade, thereby reducing his ability to blockade the French Atlantic ports.

The next part of the plan was to swiftly return across the Atlantic, join forces with other French squadrons and some 25 Spanish ships from El Ferrol and Cadiz. This combined force would then destroy Cornwallis's hopefully much-depleted fleet and sail freely en masse up the Channel to support the invasion by the *Armée de l'Angleterre* (Army of England) crossing from Boulogne. In theory, the plan was excellent, but from the outset it was flawed, mainly because it was over complicated. And although Bonaparte proved a highly capable strategist on the continent, he failed to understand that naval fleets did not move like battalions of soldiers in the field. Ships, constrained by their reliance on the wind, left far too much margin for error. There were eight successive plans.

## Bonaparte's invasion plans, 1804

**Plan 1** Authorised on 2 July 1804, this committed the French Mediterranean fleet at Toulon to sail for Rochefort, Cherbourg and thence to Boulogne. This plan was cancelled when the fleet commander Admiral Latouche-Tréville died.

**Plan 2** Authorised on 29 September 1804, it was foiled by circumstantial counteracting forces and cancelled on 8 October 1804.

**Plan 3** Although authorised on 26 October 1804, this was not put into action until Vice-Admiral Villeneuve hoisted his flag on the 80-gun *La Bucentaure* and assumed overall command of the Toulon fleet on 19 December. Four days later, Admiral Missiessy was ordered to sail for Martinique, while Villeneuve was to sail from Toulon for South America and Surinam, to attack British possessions after which both fleets were to return to the French Channel ports.

This plan never happened. That November, Austria and Russia signed a treaty unifying a Third Coalition against France which, when fully implemented

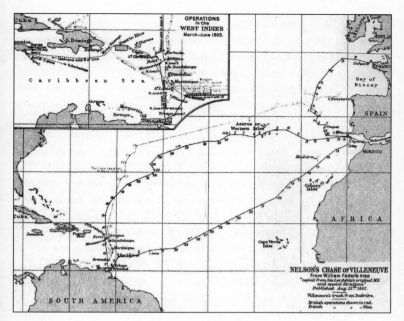

*The route taken by Nelson chasing the combined fleet across the Atlantic.*

seven months later, devastated Bonaparte's true hopes of invasion. In December, the Russo-Austro alliance was further supported when King Gustav IV of Sweden signed a secret military pact with England. On 2 December 1804, Bonaparte was crowned Emperor Napoleon I in the Cathedral of Notre-Dame, Paris. On 19 December Spain declared war on England.

## Bonaparte's invasion plans, 1805

Now a sovereign head of state, Bonaparte wrote to George III on 2 January 1805, offering a peace proposal that read: '*My dear Brother by Providence and the suffrage of the Senate, the People and the Army my foremost and most earnest desire has been for peace.*' Replying on the King's behalf, Pitt declined. Despite Bonaparte's ability to wage war on behalf of France, history does show that Bonaparte did, on many occasions, try to negotiate peace with the European powers. Finding himself continually politically blocked at every avenue,

Bonaparte was unfortunately forced to retaliate in a defensive manner. When first defeated in 1814 and compelled to abdicate, he should have capitulated, accepting exile graciously but, as Emperor, Napoleon could not forsake his beloved France. On 4 January, France and Spain signed a naval pact, providing Bonaparte with more ships to support the French navy and, using this to his advantage, he changed his strategy.

**Plan 4** Authorised on 16 January 1805, in this plan French squadrons from Brest and Rochefort were to unite with Spanish ships from El Ferrol and sail for the West Indies. Joined there by Villeneuve's squadron from Toulon, the united fleets were to attack British West Indies possessions, then return to Western Europe, to Boulogne. On 24 January, England declared war on Spain and although Missiessy had sailed from Rochefort, this plan failed for two reasons:

1. Evading Nelson's blockading squadron Villeneuve sailed from Toulon on 18 January, but was forced to return into port after storms had ravaged his ships.

2. Even though Rear-Admiral Missiessy did escape from Rochefort, reaching Martinique on 22 February, Villeneuve failed to arrive. Totally unsupported and powerless to make a strike, Missiessy sailed for France on 28 March, missing new orders to remain in the West Indies.

**Plan 5** Authorised on 27 February and 2 March, Bonaparte overturned his orders of 16 January and ordered Admiral Ganteaume to sail from Rochefort to unite with French and Spanish ships at El Ferrol, then sail to support Missiessy off Martinique. At the same time, Villeneuve was to sail from Toulon for Martinique. Bonaparte had equally ordered Ganteaume to take complete command of the Franco-Spanish forces in the West Indies and lead the entire combined fleet back to the English Channel with the intention of arriving off Boulogne between 10 June and 10 July 1805. The change in command of the combined fleet implies that Bonaparte was beginning to lose faith in Villeneuve. Plan 5 was aborted on 22 March and Missiessy sailed from Martinique for France six days later.

**Plan 6** Authorised on 30 March, this revision completely omitted the complex ruse to attack the West Indies. This time, Villeneuve was to sail for Ireland and land troops, then sail directly to Boulogne. Despite Plan 6 being retracted on

13 April, Villeneuve had already evaded Nelson's watching inshore squadron and sailed from Toulon with 11 sail of the line on 30 March.

**Plan 7** Authorised on 3 April, this strategy reverted to Bonaparte's earlier concept. Villeneuve was to sail for the West Indies, where he would be joined by Admiral Ganteaume's ships from Brest and Admiral Gravina's Spanish squadron from Cadiz. All three squadrons were to unite at Martinique with Villeneuve in overall command, to attack and seize British West Indies colonies; the entire deception drawing ships away from Cornwallis's blockading fleet defending the Western Approaches. Afterwards the combined fleet was to return to El Ferrol and thence Boulogne. This plan was superseded.

**Plan 8** Authorised on 26 July, this ordered Villeneuve to return to Europe, stopping to unite with the Spanish ships in Cadiz and El Ferrol, unite with Admiral Allemand's squadron from Rochefort and French ships from Brest then advance to Boulogne. Plan 8 was foiled by three factors:

1. The French ships failed to get out of Brest and Rochefort due to Cornwallis's tight blockade.

2. The unforeseen attack on Villeneuve's combined fleet by Admiral Robert Calder off El Ferrol on 22 July had made Villeneuve cautious.

3. Villeneuve had mishandled the situation and although he perhaps rightfully proceeded to take the combined fleet south to the safety of Cadiz to keep his fleet intact, this decision unfortunately antagonised his Emperor who was already being thwarted by other events.

## Failure of the French fleet

As described above, whichever part of the French fleet, at Brest or Rochefort, commanded by Missiessy or Ganteaume, each at some point was unable to escape or fully unite with Villeneuve and support the various modifications introduced into Bonaparte's overall invasion plan. The overall organisational breakdown, not only indicates the dogged abilities of the British Admirals Cornwallis and Nelson; the French admirals do appear to have been either reluctant or less spirited. However, these same French naval officers and their ship's commanders were to fight with gallant honour when tested at Trafalgar, as did the officers of the Spanish Navy. And although Admiral Denis Decrès, Bonaparte's Minister of Marine, appointed in October 1801, proved highly competent in executing his orders, even he was unable to manage the complexities of fleet co-operation when wind, sea state and weather were the finite deciding factors governing ship movement. Although the same issues applied to the British, the Admiralty at Whitehall proved highly capable.

## Bonaparte's revised plan

Authorised on 16 September, this completely new scheme was generated by two key factors:

1. Bonaparte's cancellation of the invasion of England;
2. His need to react to the new theatre of war developing in middle Europe.

The plan ordered the combined Franco-Spanish fleet to sail from Cadiz into the Mediterranean for deployment off Genoa. Frustrated by Villeneuve's apparent failings, Bonaparte instructed Admiral François Étienne de Rosily-Mesros to relieve Villeneuve of his command. On 28 September, Nelson assumed command of the now reinforced Mediterranean fleet lying off Cadiz. Although Rosily was now travelling south to Cadiz, Villeneuve complied with his initial instructions and ordered the combined fleet to sail on 18 October and sail east through the Straits of Gibraltar, hopefully evading Nelson's fleet; Villeneuve knew he was taking a calculated risk.

## The prelude to battle

The *Victory* anchored off Portsmouth on 18 August and Nelson departed the ship the next day and travelled home to Merton. While lying off Portsmouth, the *Victory*'s boatswain, carpenter and gunner set about their work refitting the ship and her equipment, the carpenter '*Fitting the Admirals and Captain's Apartments, the Captain of the Fleets and different officers*'. He also repaired the 'hammock boards' that formed a solid bulwark along the sides of the poop deck. This particular feature, unfortunately erroneously not visible in the restored ship today, had been permanently fitted when the *Victory* was earlier armed with carronades on her poop.

On Friday 13 September, Nelson left his home for Portsmouth and, stopping at Guildford to change horses, he penned the following in his diary: 'at *half past ten, drove from dear dear Merton, where I left all which I hold dear in this world, to go and serve my king and country. May the great God whom I adore enable me to fulfill the expectations of my country; and if it is His good pleasure that I should return, my thanks will never cease to be offered up to His throne of mercy. If it is His good Providence to cut short my days upon in this earth, I bow with the greatest submission relying that he will protect those so dear to me, that I may leave behind. His will be done. Amen. Amen. Amen.'*

After breakfasting at the George Hotel in Portsmouth, Nelson embarked his barge at Southsea and was rowed out to the *Victory*, then anchored at St Helen's Roads off the Isle of Wight. Next morning at 8am, the *Victory* weighed anchor and in *'light airs made sail to the SSE'*.

Reporting the occasion on 16 September, the *Times* commented: *'It is a circumstance not unworthy of remark, in connection with the success which has invariably attended Lord NELSON, that the wind, which has blown to the Westward and to other points, which was foul for sailing for a considerable time past, shifted on Saturday, a few minutes after his Lordship reached the Victory. At eight o'clock yesterday morning the Victory got under weigh, and by twelve she had cleared the Isle of Wight. n.b. sailing with her was the frigate Euryalus, Captain H Blackwood.*

At Plymouth on 17 September, the *Times* reported: *'Arrived this morning at eight o'clock, the Victory, of 100 guns, Vice-Admiral Lord NELSON, in company with a frigate, which he sent in to call out the ships ready here, when the Ajax and Thunderer, of 74 guns each, sailed to join him.'*

On 28 September, *Victory's* log states: *'At 10 joined the Fleet off Cadiz under the Command of Vice Admiral Collingwood.'* It was Nelson's forty-seventh birthday and 15 commanding officers were invited to dine in celebration. During this gathering Nelson revealed his battle plan. His intention was to attack the combined fleet at right angles, with his ships formed in three columns of ships to divide the enemy line of battle. Unconventional but simple, this method had been used successfully by Admiral George Rodney at the Battle of the Saintes in 1782, with the concept inspired by an amateur Scots tactician, John Eldin.

Very little happened in the *Victory* for the next few weeks. Villeneuve, safe in Cadiz, was having problems provisioning; manning the ships also proved difficult due to an endemic outbreak of yellow fever. Matters were not helped when, holding a Conseil de Guerre on 8 October, some of his French and Spanish captains revolted. Despite this tribulation, Villeneuve ordered his fleet to sail for Italy as planned. On Saturday 18 October, the *Victory* received signals from *Euryalus's* inshore squadron revealing that Villeneuve's combined fleet was hoisting and crossing their yards ready to sail. At this point the *Victory* and Nelson's battle fleet were cruising 50 miles to seaward of Cadiz; signals being relayed via the *Colossus, Defence* and *Mars*. The next day the *Victory's* log records that they had '*Shifted the Main Top Sail*', Captain Hardy adding that he had metered out '*punishment to ten seamen with 36 lashes each, all for drunkenness*'. Within 48 hours these men would be in battle. Shortly after, the *Victory* received *Euryalu*s's signal '*the Enemy is putting out to sea*'.

## The Battle of Cape Trafalgar, 21 October 1805

While there are many accounts of the battle in its entirety, the following simply applies from the perspective of Nelson's flagship, the *Victory*. As dawn broke on Monday 21 October the sea state was a heavy swell from the west. The *Victory's* log for Tuesday 22 October commences: '*Light Airs and Cloudy Standing towards the Enemy Van, with all Sails set, At 4 Minutes past 12 opened our Fire on the Enemys Van in passing down their Line At 12.20 In attempting to pass through their Line fell on board the 10ᵗʰ & 11ᵗʰ Ships when the action became General.*' (As ship's time starts at 12 noon ship's journals actually read one day ahead.)

As the *Victory* crossed *Le Bucentaure's* stern, she fired her larboard 68-pounder carronade loaded with one round of shot and a canister of 500 muskets balls. Followed by every broadside gun as it bore, the blast from the *Victory's* double-shotted volley swathed mercilessly straight through the crowded decks of the French flagship, dealing death and destruction in its wake and rendering her into a powerless wreck. Twenty guns were dismounted and some 325 Frenchmen fell dead or disabled. While the *Victory* fired at Villeneuve's flagship, she unavoidably ran alongside *Le Redoubtable's* larboard side and, getting entangled, the two ships drifted to leeward. Both ships fought ferociously, the British seamen manning *Victory's* starboard battery dashing buckets of water out through the ports as they fired their guns to prevent the burning wads from setting *Le Redoubtable* ablaze. During this gunnery duel a fire broke out in the *Victory's* cockpit near a hanging magazine. It would have exploded with devastating consequences to the entire ship had not Midshipman Carslake rapidly extinguished the flames.

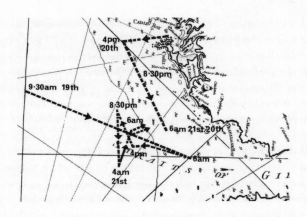

*The position of the British and combined Franco-Spanish fleets
on the morning of the Battle of Trafalgar.*

*Nelson's Trafalgar battle plan*

Fire in this vicinity was a disastrous situation that might have led to the destruction of the *Victory* as happened to the French 120-gun ship *L'Orient* at Nelson's Battle of the Nile in 1798. The sudden loss of the *Victory* would have had a profound effect on the ensuing battle; besides the loss of life and firepower, the morale of the whole of Nelson's fleet could have been broken.

Well trained by *Le Redoubtable's* commander Captain Jean Jacques Lucas, the French crew retained a ferocious fusillade of musketry fire from their main, fore and mizzen tops onto the decks of the *Victory*, most were directed towards the quarterdeck, the nerve centre of the ship. Lucas's men also lobbed over 200 grenades, their sharp explosions scattering the *Victory's* defenders for cover and causing more casualties. Small fires also broke out on the *Victory's* forecastle but were soon extinguished. Amid the affray Nelson and Hardy paced the quarterdeck then, as they turned by the hatchway, tragedy stuck: The *Victory's* log records that '*About 1.15 the Right Hon^{ble}. Lord Visc^t. Nelson K.B. and Commander in Chief was wounded in the shoulder.*'

Hit by a musket ball fired from *Le Redoubtable's* mizzen top, Nelson fell to his knees on the spot where his secretary Scott had fallen earlier. Instantly Marine Sergeant Secker, Able Seaman James Sharman and another rushed to support the Admiral. Nelson then told Hardy: '*They have done for me at last Hardy,*' adding, '*my backbone is shot through*'. As the Admiral was being carried below Midshipmen Pollard and Collingwood turned their muskets towards the *Le Redoubtable's* mizzen top, their volley dispatching all the Frenchmen manning it.

Although most of the *Victory's* upper-deck 12-pounders were now out of action, her larboard battery continued firing into the *Santissima Trinidad* and *Le Bucentaure*. Still entangled with the *Victory*, *Le Redoubtable* drifted southeast, colliding with Harvey's *Temeraire*. Believing the *Victory* was in difficulty, Harvey fired his larboard guns and 32-pounder carronades into Lucas's ship.

Thinking that *Le Redoubtable* was ready to surrender, the *Victory* momentarily ceased firing and although *Temeraire's* guns created more carnage on the French ship, Lucas refused to surrender and prepared to board the *Victory*. Ordering the slings of his main yard to be cut, the yard crashed down on the *Victory's* waist, forming a bridge over which hordes of French seamen clambered, while others succeeded in getting on to the *Victory's* starboard anchors. Instantaneously, Captain Charles Adair called up his marines from the *Victory's* decks below to repulse the attack. The ensuing skirmish was bloody: 19 officers and men were killed and 22 wounded; Adair himself was fatally shot through his neck by a musket ball. For a brief moment it appeared that the *Victory* would be overwhelmed but *Temeraire's* carronades soon obliterated the enemy boarders with grape shot.

Reopening fire, Lieutenants Williams, King Yule and Brown ordered *Victory's* guns to be depressed and loaded with reduced charges to prevent shot passing through *Le Redoubtable* into *Le Temeraire*. The *Victory's* treble-shotted guns ripped into *Le Redoubtable*, penetrating her orlop and starting fires. Totally crippled and with rising casualties *Le Redoubtable* finally capitulated.

The capture of *Le Redoubtable* had been hard earned. According to the *Victory's* log, '*at 1.30 the Redoubtable having Struck her Colours we ceased firing our Starboard Guns but continued engaged with the Santissima Trinidad and some of the Enemy's Ships on the Larboard Side Observed the Temeraire between the Redoubtable and another French Ship of the Line both of which had Struck – the Action continued General until 3 o'clock when several of the Enemy's Ships around had Struck – Observed the Royal Sovereign with the Loss of her Main and Mizen Masts and several of the Enemy Ships around her dismasted At 3.30 Observed 4 Sail of the Enemy's Van, Tack and stand along our Weather Line to Windward fired our Larboard Guns at those that would reach At 3.40 made the Signal for out Ships to keep their Wind and engage the Enemys Van coming along our Weather Line – At 4.15 – The Spanish Rear Admiral to Windward Struck to some of our ships, which had Tacked after them*'. The Spanish ship referred to was the *Santa Ana*.

On the *Victory's* orlop Chevalier, Nelson's servant, fearing that the Admiral was near to death, summoned the surgeon, Beatty. While Beatty took Nelson's hand and felt his pulse and cold forehead, the Admiral opened his eyes briefly, then peacefully closed them. Again, the surgeon left to help the wounded but after five minutes when Beatty was recalled, Chevalier announced that '*he believed his Lordship had expired.*' It was 4.30pm, at which time, according to Beatty, Nelson died.

The *Victory's* log continues: '*Observed one of the Enemy's Ships blow up and 14 sail of the Enemys' Ships standing to the Southward – Partial Firing continued untill 3.40 when a Victory having been reported to the Right Hon*<sup>ble</sup>. *Viscount Lord Nelson K.B. and Commander in Chief he died of his Wound ... At 5 the Mizen Mast fell about 10 feet above the Poop The Lower Masts, Yards, and Bowsprit all crippled –*

*Rigging and Sails very much cut – The Ships around us much crippled Several of our Ships pursuing the Enemy to Leeward Saw Vice Admiral Collingwoods flag flying on board H.M. Ship Euryalus and some of our ships taking Possession of the Prizes – Struck Top Gall'. Mats, Got up runners and tackles to secure the Lower Masts Employed clearing the Wrecks of the Yards and rigging – Wore Ship and Sounded in 32 fm Sandy Bottom – Stood to the Southward under the Remnants of the Fore sails and Mizen Top Sail, Sounded from 13 to 19 fm. At 2 Wore Ship At Day Light Saw our Fleet and Prizes 43 sail in Sight still closing with our Fleet – At 6 cape Trafalgar bore SEbE Dist. 4 or 5 Leagues – At 6.30 Saw 3 of the Enemy's Ships to Leeward standing towards Cadiz Fresh Breezes and Cloudy – Employed Knotting the fore and main Rigging and Fishing and securing the Lower Masts Struck the Fore Top Mast for a Fish for the Fore mast which was very badly wounded – at Noon Fresh Breezes and Hazy.'*

Casualties on the *Victory* were high, 54 dead, rising to 57, with three men dying of their wounds later. As for the wounded, the final number was 102 as 27 more men reported to Beatty after he made his official return of 75.

## The storm

Regardless of the rising storm, work continued on returning the *Victory* to a seaworthy state. On Wednesday 23 October, the seamen, *'bent a Fore Sail for a Main Sail, the old Main Sail Shot all to Pieces…Watch employed, Woolding the Lower Masts &c. … bent a Main Top Sail old one Shot to Pieces – Got a Jib Boom up and rigged for a Jury Mizen – Employed securing the Masts, Yards and Rigging – Carpenters Employed stopping the Shot Holes &c as necessary'.*

All the while the *Victory* was making 12 inches (30cm) of water in the hold hourly and her chain pumps were continuously manned.

After *'clearing the wreck of the Mizen Mast',* on Thursday 24 October, the *Victory* encountered: *'Strong Gales and Heavy Squalls with rain and a Heavy Sea from the West … At 11 HM Ship Polyphemus took us in tow'.* Still, *'Setting up the fore Rigging',* on Friday, they *'Got up a Jurry Fore Top Mast and a Main Top Gall'. Yard for a Fore Top Sail Yard and bent the Mizen Top Sail for a Fore Top Sail … At 9.20 Wore, Observed a Ship on Fire astern, At 9.45 she blew up.'*

This could have been one of two prizes, *L'Intrépide* or *San Augustin*, which being unable to endure the storm had to be burnt. Alternatively, it was either *L'Indomptable* or *El Rayo* that went ashore and burned.

On Saturday 26 October, *Victory* suffered badly in the storm: '*At 4.15 Heavy Squalls, At 5.10 Carried away the Main Yard – Split the Main Top Sail and Main Sail all to Pieces … Polyphemus increased her Distance from us Supposing the Hawser had Parted – Hard Gales and a Heavy Swell from the WSW Bent a Fore sail and Set the main Stay Sail*'.

With her tow rope parted, the *Victory* was now left to her own devices. Next morning Hardy recorded that '*seaman Henry Cramwell (S) died of his battle wound and the Africa was seen with all her masts gone sending distress signals*'. After setting up a jury main yard and fitting the main topsail yard, the *Neptune* took the *Victory* in tow. Also on that Sunday, James Gordon, one of the *Victory's* 31 boys, died of his wounds. Still off Trafalgar, on Monday 28 October, the *Victory's* ordeal was not over; again the tow rope parted and the *Neptune*, '*Carried away her Fore Top Mast*'. Finally reaching Gibraltar on Tuesday 29 October (log time), the *Victory* anchored in Rosia Bay at 7am. Next morning, Midshipman Palmer died from his wounds.

# 16

# SAWBONES AND SICK BERTH

## FIT FOR SERVICE

Keeping the *Victory's* crew in good health was essential for running a man-of-war efficiently. Men needed to be fit for operating rigging and sails, manning the yards aloft and, most importantly to be in prime condition to fight when the ship was brought into action. Sea battles at this period were not won by good ship handling, seamanship and gunnery alone, they were equally won by keeping the crew healthy. Health could only be maintained by providing a nutritious diet high in calories, the introduction of preventative medicine and establishing good hygiene practices. Nelson himself said, '*The great thing in all military service is health and you will agree with me that it is easier for an officer to keep men healthy, than for a physician to cure them.*'

### Causes of death

At the beginning of the war with Revolutionary France in 1793 some 42 per cent of deaths in the Georgian Navy were caused by disease, compared with an average of 3–5 per cent in battle. This does not mean that higher casualties couldn't be sustained in action; it depended on the ferocity of the engagement. When attacking Fort Moultrie on 28 June 1776, the *Bristol* lost 11 per cent of her crew. At Trafalgar, the *Victory*, suffering the highest number of British casualties, only had 7 per cent of crew killed, while the 98-gun *Prince* suffered none.

### Accidental deaths

The number of deaths from daily accidents in the Royal Navy seems remarkably low when taking into account the frequency with which large numbers of men had to work aloft. While most falls from the rigging did incur serious injuries, analysis shows that on average one man on each ship died annually from such accidents. Such reality is supported by Captain Berry's account when commanding Nelson's earlier flagship, the 74-gun *Vanguard,* in 1798. After enduring a terrible storm off Genoa in May that year Berry wrote to his father-in-law: *'before 12 at night the gale came on, and increased with rapid violence, which obliged us to furl all the sails and try under a main storm-staysail. At about two, the main-topmast went over the side, with the top-sail yard full of men. I dreaded the inquiry of who were killed and drowned; fortunately only one man fell overboard, and one fell on the booms, and was killed on the spot.'*

## Common injuries or deaths

Most deaths or injuries related to accidents generated by the ship's motion in heavy seas. They included men falling down ladders or being thrown against parts of the ship's fittings, burns and scalds suffered by cooks or ship's boats being overturned. Hernias, caused by lifting and heaving extremely heavy weights without mechanical aids, were very common; seamen suffering with such being issued with trusses. Other injuries at sea were usually caused by neglect or ignorance. Accidentally falling overboard was quite common and although it has been suggested that most sailors could not swim, about 35 per cent of those that went into the sea were recovered alive. Should the victim be partially drowned, the surgeon would treat him with a strong onion broth that was thought to help prevent bronchitis or other inflammatory lung problems.

## Suicide

This was extremely rare in the Georgian Navy simply because it did not conform to normal behaviour and common religious conviction within Georgian society. An isolated case related to Able Seaman William Maynard who *'Was found hanging in the Bread Room'*, on board Nelson's earlier command, the 28-gun sixth-rate frigate *Albemarle*, on Sunday 18 March 1781. The ship's logbook provides no clue as to why Maynard took his life; more tragic is the fact that this occurred at Woolwich after the ship had returned home from the West Indies.

## Disease

Warships of this period were densely populated, with most of the crew living confined on gun decks. Most problems for naval surgeons such as the *Victory's* Beatty and his assistants were caused by outbreaks of contagious diseases. If not isolated, a disease such as prison fever could sweep through the ship, devastating the entire crew. In home waters, typhus was a major concern, while for ships operating in tropical climates malaria, yellow fever, tropical sprue and other debilitating disorders were rife. With the exception of malaria, most diseases caused gastro-intestinal infections that brought about diarrhoea, dehydration, fever, melancholy and weakness.

The speed with which these diseases could reduce a crew is evident from the daily records given in the logbook of Captain Cuthbert Collingwood's 28-gun sixth-rate frigate *Hinchinbrook*. On taking over command of the ship from Captain Nelson on 1 May 1780 Collingwood wrote, '*the ship is very leaky, and 70 men with fevers: John Stockbridge departed this life.*' Making matters worse, the surgeon's mate, James Hugggins died the next day. Between 1 May and 8 September Collingwood was to lose 124 men (62 per cent of 200 crew). Efforts at prevention were made by sending the fit men on shore to erect tents into which the sick were removed. Following this, the *Hinchinbrook's* surgeon set about setting the crew to wash '*the ship with Vinegar*', vinegar being used as a disinfectant; they also fumigated the ship by setting up, '*fire in iron pots continuously burning on the lower deck*', each of which would have contained brimstone (sulphur). So debilitated were the *Hinchinbrook's* crew that seamen from accompanying ships undertook getting water and wood, and later assisted in sailing the ship back to Port Royal, Jamaica.

## An outbreak of typhus on board the *Elephant*

The epidemic on board the *Elephant* at anchor in Spithead in October 1790 reveals the measures undertaken by surgeons in order to treat viruses. Although Captain Thompson's logbook does not specify the disease prevailing in his ship, it does show that 11 per cent of the crew found infected were removed from the ship directly to the naval hospital at Haslar within the first week.

Thompson's journal also clearly describes the orderly procedure of dealing with disease-ridden ships. The first measures taken were to move the *Elephant* alongside the hulk *Goliath*, an out-of-commission ship used for accommodation, before undertaking a systematic procedure to eliminate all sources of the disease. While more men were sent to hospital, the remaining crew methodically washed the ship throughout with vinegar and fumigated each deck using tobacco smoke as an alternative to burning brimstone or gunpowder. To do this effectively, all gun ports had to be shut. All potential sources of disease, including filthy shingle ballast that was often the cause for fevers, were heaved out of the *Elephant* during this cleaning process.

As for the men, all were systematically removed mess by mess to the *Goliath* where they could be thoroughly washed without contamination and had their clothes fumigated with tobacco. In all, 146 men, 27 per cent of the *Elephant's* ship's company, were sent to Haslar. This example shows that captains and surgeons undertook every conceivable measure to eradicate the threat of disease.

| Procedures undertaken in the **Elephant** *to combat disease* | |
|---|---|
| **Day and date** | **Task** |
| Thursday 7 October | 'Breaking the up hold, starting the water and sending casks onshore' |
| Friday 8 October | 'Fumigated the ship with brimstone thrown over Charcoal fires' |
| Saturday 9 October | 'Employed as before and shifted the Provisions & Wood into the Hulk' |
| Sunday 10 October | 'Fumigated as before, and washed with vinegar' |
| Tuesday 12 October | 'Employed as before … employed getting the Guns out' |
| Wednesday 13 October | 'Employed getting the Guns out, and the Cables into the Hulk' |
| Thursday 14 October | 'Employed getting the shingle ballast out, and the stores, and wood into the Hulk' |
| Saturday 16 October | 'Employed getting the ballast out' |
| Sunday 17 October | 'Employed discharging the ballast total quantity 316 tons. Fumigating the ship and washed with vinegar. Also washed 20 messes of the Ship's Company and shifted them with purified cloaths a place set apart in the Hulk for fumigating the men's cloaths with tobacco' |
| Monday 18 October | 'Fumigated the Ship and washed with vinegar as before' |
| Tuesday 19 October | 'Washed the remainder of the Ship's Company and shifted them as before … shifted all hands into the Hulk' |
| Wednesday 20 October | 'Came on board the Riggers and warped the ship down the jetty for docking, fumigated with tobacco' |
| Thursday 21 October | 'A gang of hands on board the Ship. fumigated the hulk w[th] tobacco' |

## The advent of the sick berth

The great advances made in naval medicine at the end of the eighteenth century were influenced by three physicians: Sir Gilbert Blane, James Lind and Thomas Trotter. Under their leadership, naval surgeons acquired a far better understanding of diseases and their prevention. Initiatives were also taken up by ship's commanders to assist them in combating the problem of contagion. It had long been the practice to move the sick to one separate area of the deck where the main body of the crew lived, with the result that infection would continue to spread.

The first documented attempt to provide better facilities for tending to the sick relates to Captain John Markham of the 74-gun ship HMS *Centaur* which served with the Mediterranean fleet in 1798. Markham moved his sick berth from the lower deck to an area on the upper gun deck under the starboard side of the forecastle. The area created provided a segregated 'ward' containing some 22 beds or cots, the former for those with broken limbs; the foremost end by the beakhead bulkhead contained a day-use dispensary and table, the main dispensary itself was down below on the orlop beside the surgeon's cabin. The concept was not entirely new: John Knyveton, a surgeon's mate who served during the Seven Year's War (1756–1763), recalled in his diary, *Surgeon's Mate,* that the sick berth in his ship was sited under the forecastle. Welcoming Markham's idea, Admiral Sir John Jervis issued the following directive to his fleet, '*The Commander in Chief positively directs that no sick are to be kept below the upper deck in any line of battle ship under his command, and that a sick berth is to be prepared in each* [ship] *under the forecastel [sic] on the starboard side with a roundhouse enclosed for the sick*'; the roundhouse being an enclosed toilet or 'head'.

While some complied, this order met some criticism because livestock had to be moved elsewhere to facilitate the sick berth, one ship complaining that the removal of their hog-sty caused '*the swine to range the main deck to the annoyance of the men*'. Both Knyveton and Markham found the revised location under the forecastle provided many advantages:

1. Plenty of light and fresh air.

2. Having a segregated toilet facility built in the beakhead bulkhead prevented contagion being transferred from the sick to healthy crew members.

3. Being near the ship's galley stove there was a plentiful supply of hot water and warmth, likewise hot broth could be easily administered to the ill.

A sick berth based on the above information sources has been reconstructed below the *Victory's* forecastle and furnished for visitor interpretation.

## The prevention of scurvy

Throughout most of the eighteenth century scurvy was the most debilitating disease suffered by seamen. It arose mainly from the poor and unbalanced diet resulting from the limited number of foodstuffs that could be carried at sea without deterioration. The problem was exacerbated by the conservative attitudes to food from the seamen themselves, resenting anything different even if it was introduced in their best interests. Surgeons, working in unison with the ship's captain and purser, took every opportunity to combat scurvy by providing the ship's company with a more balanced diet, including fresh vegetables and sufficient vitamin C from lemons and limes as recommended by Blane and Lind, supported by earlier trials undertaken by pioneers such as Captain James Cook and Lieutenant William Bligh.

# THE SURGEON IN BATTLE

Besides treating tropical disease, daily injuries, ailments and venereal disease, ship's surgeons and assistants also had to cope with battle casualties. Wounds would include those caused by missiles, bullets and splinters, penetration wounds, burns, compound fractures, concussion and shock. Working under extreme conditions with little assistance, the naval surgeon had to assess and resolve the severity of each injury presented to him. He also had to be decisive about which casualties would benefit from an operation and which would die anyway, what would today be called 'triaging'.

For example, when Nelson was fatally wounded at Trafalgar, Dr Beatty knew the Admiral was beyond any practical surgery and he was therefore made as comfortable as possible before he died. Beatty wrote, '*His Lordship was requested by the surgeon to make him acquainted with all sensations*' He replied that, '*he felt a gushing of blood every minute within his breast: that he had no feeling in the lower part of his body: and that his breathing was difficult, and attended with very severe pain about that part of spine where he was confident that the ball had struck; for, said he, 'I felt it break my back'. These symptoms but more particularly, the gush of blood which His Lordship complained of, together with the state of pulse, indicated to the Surgeon the hopeless situation of the case.*'

As in warfare today, the surgeon accepted the fact that most abdominal wounds were fatal and that comfort and compassion were all that could be offered, with the assistance of the ship's chaplain.

## Missile injuries

These wounds were caused by round shot, chain and bar shot, grape shot, musket and pistol shot. Being smaller, musket and pistol balls could, if they did not shatter the bone, be entirely removed using specially designed extractors, the ball being held by the muscles surrounding it going into spasm. It was the weight and velocity of the larger projectiles that inflicted horrendous wounds. Besides decapitation or taking off the limbs of victims, it was when these projectiles sliced away portions of flesh and muscle from the victim, or shattered their bones that surgeons were presented with the most serious problems. Where flesh only had been removed the surgeon could do little but staunch bleeding and stitch the casualty together as best he could. The alternative was amputation.

## Splinter wounds

According to surgeon Alexander Hutchison, these were created by '*ragged fragments of timber violently rent from the planks or sides of the ship, by round shot*'. He further stated, '*Wounds inflicted by splinters of wood are always more extensive, accompanied with frightful contusions and lacerations of the soft parts.*'

Splinters were generally removed using probes after removing the skin with an implement known as a fleam, the wound being sewn up on completion. The major problem that occurred with splinter wounds was tetanus. It was therefore essential that all matter within the wound be removed with probes before infection took hold. Badly lacerated splinter wounds often led to amputation which, though traumatic, was quicker than attempting to recover the limb.

## Penetration wounds

Caused by pikes, cutlasses, bayonets and hatchets, these were dealt with according to the severity of the wound or its proximity to internal organs. While wounds caused by the former three weapons were generally inflicted on the torso and arms, hatchet wounds were mainly confined to the head, face and shoulders; whichever the case, the main objective was to stop the haemorrhaging by suture or pressure bandaging.

Where internal bleeding could not be stemmed it was customary to lower blood pressure by bloodletting, to allow the blood to clot.

## Amputations

Because of the number of compound fractures and traumatic avulsions (severing of limbs), naval surgeons such as Beatty had to operate with speed and efficiency because they had no real means of anaesthetising patients during an operation. As a result, they were capable of performing a complete amputation in one and a half minutes, sometimes less.

The patient's skin was washed and shaved beforehand if time permitted. Next the patient was anaesthetised with laudanum or an opiate and given a pad of leather to bite on. The belief that the victim was given rum or other spirits is incorrect. This practice was actually avoided because alcohol thinned the blood and preventing it from clotting. If an operation was to be successful it was essential that the blood clotted otherwise the casualty might later bleed to death. Then tourniquets were applied, which provided temporary localised anaesthesia to the limb being cut.

Next, with a few rapid sweeps of a 'capital' knife, a circular cut was made around the limb below the wound. The resultant flap of skin was then peeled back above the point of amputation. Using either an amputation saw or knife, the surgeon then cut though the bone. Next the tourniquets were eased and bleeding blood vessels were clinched with forceps, while the surgeon then applied sutures, possibly silk ligatures, to seal all blood vessels.

Finally the flap of skin was stitched over to close the stump and the entire wound was sealed with oil of turpentine which acted as a disinfectant. The common surgical practice of the time was to leave the ends of all ligatures long and draw them out through the wound so that they acted as a drain for the infective discharges that almost invariably occurred. This enabled ready removal when they separated naturally. After the operation, the victim would be given more laudanum or opium to ease the trauma as the original anesthetic wore off, but a draught of spirits or wine to ease the pain would have been more common. When Nelson had his arm amputated in 1797 the wound was treated using saline solution and dressed with '*calamine and dry lint*'.

Although singular amputations were common, one surgeon, Ralph Cumming, successfully undertook the first ever four-quarter amputation in the naval hospital at Antigua in 1808. His patient had had his arm torn away at the shoulder by a round shot from a fort at Guadaloupe. So extensive were the injuries that Cumming was obliged to remove the remains of the arm, together with the collarbone and shoulder blade. Not only was this a highly complicated operation demanding an expert knowledge of anatomy, it equally involved suturing many blood vessels. Although terribly scarred the sailor made a full recovery and later reported to Greenwich Hospital to claim his pension. Cumming was not so fortunate, he died shortly afterwards of yellow fever.

## Burns

Fire and explosion presented a far greater hazard to the ships and men of the Nelsonian period than round shot. Despite great precautions to confine gunpowder safely in the magazines, in battle the many cartridges being conveyed to the guns in their 'cases of wood' could easily be ignited, with the resultant explosion and flash fires leading to scorch injuries. Another common source of burns came from firing guns using slow-match where the flash from the powder spread at the touch hole could prove risky. Because this kind of wound affected some 25 per cent of the gunners, surgeons, as well as gunnery officers, campaigned for the universal introduction of flint-operated gunlocks. As a result, the number of flash burns caused by firing virtually disappeared. Burns were treated by applying the *'lintseed oil'* that was carried by dispensaries for a number of uses. The alternative practice was to use urine, a sterile liquid.

The intensity of dealing with the wounded in action is vividly portrayed in the account of Surgeon Robert Young who served in the 64-gun *Ardent* during the ferocious Battle of Camperdown against the Dutch on 11 October 1797. Having no surgeon's mate to assist him, Young had to work alone: *'I was employed operating and dressing till 4.0 in the morning, the action beginning at 1.0 in the afternoon. So great was my fatigue that I began several amputations under a dread of sinking before I had secured the blood vessels.*

*Ninety wounded were brought down during the action. The whole cockpit deck, cabins, wing berths and part of the cable tier, together with my platform and preparations for dressing were covered with them. So that for a time they were laid on each other at the foot of the ladder where they were brought own, and I was obliged to go on deck to the Commanding Officer to state the situation and apply for men to go down the min hatchway and move the foremost wounded further forward into the tiers and wings and thus make more room in the cockpit. Numbers, about 16, mortally wounded, died after they were brought down, amongst whom was Captain Burgess, whose corpse could with difficulty be conveyed to the starboard wing berth. Joseph Bonheur had his right thigh taken off by a cannon shot close to the pelvis, so that it was impossible to apply a tourniquet; his right arm was also shot to pieces. The stun of the thigh, which was very fleshy, presented a large and dreadful surface of mangled flesh. In this state he lived near two hours, perfectly sensible and incessantly calling out in a strong voice to me to assist him. The bleeding from the femoral artery, although so high up, must have been inconsiderable, and I observed it did not bleed as he lay.'*

Consistently disturbed in his work, Young recalled that, *'Melancholy cries for assistance were addressed to me from every side by the wounded and dying, and piteous moans and bewailing from pain and despair. In the midst of these agonising scenes, I was able to … direct my attention where the greatest and most essential services could be performed. Some with wounded, bad indeed and painful but slight in comparison with the dreadful condition of others, were most vociferous for my assistance. These I was obliged to reprimand with severity, as their voices disturbed the last moments of the dying. I cheered and commended the patient fortitude of others, and sometimes extorted a smile of satisfaction from the mangled sufferers, and succeeded to throw momentary gleams of cheerfulness among so many horrors. The man whose leg I first amputated had not uttered a groan from the time he was brought down, and several, exulting in the news of victory, declared they regretted not the loss of their limbs.'*

Young was also distracted by an unforeseeable but typical battle-related event: *'An explosion of a salt box with several cartridges abreast of the cockpit hatchway filled the hatchway with flame and in a moment 14 or 15 wretches tumbled down upon each other, their faces black as a cinder, their clothes blown to shatters and their hats on fire. A Corporal of Marines lived two hours after the action with all the gluteal muscles shot away, so as to excavate the pelvis. Captain Burgess' wound was of this nature but fortunately he died almost instantly.'*

In conclusion, Young wrote: *'After the action ceased, 16 or 17 dead bodies were removed before it was possible to get the platform cleared and come at the materials for operating and dressing, those I had prepared being covered over with bodies and blood, and the store room door blocked up. I have the satisfaction to say that those who survived to undergo amputation or dressed, all were found next morning in the gunroom where they were placed in as comfortable state as possible, and on the third day they were conveyed on shore in good spirits, cheering the ship at going away.'*

## Attending the sick and wounded

Under normal circumstances the *Victory's* surgeon Dr Beatty and his assistants dealt with patients in the dedicated sick berth, undertaking periodic 'rounds' or receiving fresh cases daily. Also attending were loblolly boys who acted as untrained 'nurses' and dealt with feeding the sick and their toiletry needs.

However, in battle things were different; first the sick berth and its accessories were totally removed (patients included) as the area was rapidly transformed into a fighting part of the upper gun deck. At the same time, the surgeon's mates and loblolly boys set up an action emergency theatre down below in the dim confines of the orlop or platform in the hold of a single-gun-decked ship – i.e. a frigate. Also ready in attendance were the chaplain, the purser, valets and other non-combatants. Possibly wearing the 'black operating smock' commonly used at that time, the surgeon laid out his surgical instruments: amputation saws and knives, torniquets, fleams (razor-edged flaying knifes) and probes to remove splinters, bullet extractors, ligatures to bind arteries, needle and sutures to stitch up wounds, forceps and tweezers. His assistants set out buckets of water for washing wounds and surgical instruments, empty buckets for 'wings and limbs' and tore up linen for bandages. Vinegar was used for disinfecting, and oil of turpentine to seal limb stumps.

Canvas and bedding were then spread along the wings of the orlop for the wounded to lie on while awaiting the services of the surgeon. Although naval surgeons could deal with most injuries, they had no antibiotics to prevent infection setting in after surgery and it was not uncommon to find that some casualties died after successful operations, for regardless of the surgeon's skill it was during aftercare that problems arose. Men could either die from loss of blood or be so traumatised by pain that they lost the will to live. Every endeavour was made to transfer the wounded out of the ship into hospital ships accompanying the fleet or land on shore to be admitted to one of the various naval hospitals. Many of the Trafalgar wounded, including men from the *Victory* were landed in the hospital at Gibraltar, some later dying. A gravestone reads:
*To the memory of Captain Thomas Norman of the Royal Marine Corps [who] suferd [sic] several Weeks with Patience & Fortitude and the Effects of a Severe Wound receivd [sic] in the great & memorable Seafight off Trafalgar ...*

# 17

# NELSON, HERO OF THE *VICTORY*

*Brave Nelson gone our Hero is no more,*
*Long his sad fate, Each Briton will deplore,*
*He fel a midst, the din of wars Alarms,*
*Mourn then you Son, of Britain Mourn,*
*Your Brave Defender, that will ne'er Return,*
*He lived se the Glorious Battle wone,*
*And Resigned, his Breathe without a Grone,*
*But the Victory's ours, how dear was Bought,*
*To Rob us of a Brave a man as ever Fought,*
*Each Tar laments there Kind Commander Gone,*
*And Sting with bitter anguish there sad loss who mourn,*
*Beauty Protector Bravery Reward,*
*He died lamented as he died Adored,*
*Ye British forever bewail your conquered doom,*
*And with unfaded laurels Deck immortal Nelson's Tomb.*

TAKEN FROM THE JOURNAL OF THE *VICTORY'S* MASTER GUNNER WILLIAM RIVERS
WHO SERVED IN HMS *VICTORY* FROM 1793 TO 1812.

Through her role at Trafalgar, the *Victory* is synonymous with Admiral Horatio Lord Nelson KCB, the most celebrated naval officer of his time.

Born in Burnham Thorpe, Norfolk, England, on 29 September 1758, Horatio Nelson was the sixth of 11 children. His mother, Catherine (née Suckling) died on 24 December in 1767 leaving her husband to raise the family; his father, Edmund, was vicar of Burnham Thorpe. Nelson and his brother William were sent to King Edward VI's Grammar School in Norwich in 1767, boarding there each term. Two years later both boys attended Paston Grammar School, in neighbouring North Walsham.

## Early career

On leaving school in 1771, Nelson entered into the Royal Navy on HMS *Raisonnable* on 24 April at Sheerness, Kent, a ship commanded by his uncle Maurice Suckling. When the ship 'paid off' Nelson transferred with his uncle into the *Triumph* at Chatham. As a captain's servant Nelson had little to do so Suckling sent him into a merchant ship sailing to the West Indies.

Serving as a midshipman Nelson gained valuable experience at sea. Returning to the HMS *Triumph* 14 months later, he spent much time sailing *Triumph*'s boats around Chatham and the shoals of the Thames estuary, gaining experience that later served him well. On 4 June 1773 Nelson entered into the bomb vessel HMS *Carcass*, which sailed with the *Racehorse* on an expedition to the Arctic seeking out the North West Passage under the overall command of Constantine Phipps with Captain Skeffington Lutwidge commanding the *Carcass*. Although Nelson had an encounter with a polar bear, the voyage failed in its objective.

That October Nelson entered into the 20-gun HMS *Seahorse*, which sailed for the East Indies station. Although Nelson had his first taste of battle when the *Seahorse* was attacked by hostile Indian boats belonging to the Prince Hyder Ali, he also contracted malaria. He was so ill, that he was sent home to England in HMS *Dolphin*, almost dying on route.

Once recovered he entered into the 64-gun ship HMS *Worcester* as acting fourth lieutenant and the ship was deployed escorting convoys in the channel. Passing his lieutenant's exam, Nelson joined HMS *Lowestoffe* deployed out of Port Royal, Jamaica, undertaking blockade duties in the West Indies. During this time he captured his first prize, the American brig *Little Lucy*. In September 1778 he was appointed first lieutenant in the 44-gun HMS *Bristol*, Three months later he was promoted the rank of Commander taking command of the 12-gun brig HMS *Badger*.

## Post captain

Already showing considerable aptitude, in June 1779 Nelson was promoted to the rank of post captain in command of the 28-gun sixth-rate frigate *Hinchinbrook*. In this vessel he took part in the disastrous expedition to Fort Juan, Nicaragua, the experience of which showed him how tropical disease could affect ship's crews. Back in Port Royal, he was given command of HMS *Janus*, but too ill to take up the post he returned to England and convalesced at Bath. In August 1781 Nelson was given command of HMS *Albemarle,* escorting Baltic convoys. Gaining knowledge of the Baltic proved advantageous when he was involved in the attack on the Danish fleet at Copenhagen and watching Russian ports in 1801. The *Albemarle* was also deployed escorting convoys up the St Lawrence River to Quebec before joining Lord Hood's squadron in the West Indies. In March 1784, Nelson took command of HMS *Boreas,* sailing for Antigua in the West Indies. While on this station, Nelson befriended Captain Collingwood of the *Mediator* (later Admiral Collingwood who served with Nelson at Trafalgar). Collingwood and Nelson shared an unrequited love for Mrs Mary Moutray, the wife of the Commissioner of English Harbour, Antigua.

During the three years' deployment in the *Boreas* upholding the navigation laws and stopping and searching merchant ships, Nelson fell in love with the widow, Frances 'Fanny' Nisbit. When the couple married on the island of Nevis on 11 March 1787, the attending best man was the naval commander of the 28-gun frigate *Pegasus* Prince William Henry (later William IV) to whom Nelson had been acting as aide-de-camp. When the Treaty of Paris was signed on 3 September 1787 officially ending the American War of Independence, Nelson and his wife returned to England.

## 'On the beach'

Unemployed and on half-pay, Nelson settled in Norfolk with Fanny. Now aged 29, Nelson had become an accomplished commander operating in various locations although his duties to date had been somewhat mundane. Extensive research through many extant ship's journals reveals that most ship deployments undertaken by the Royal Navy were routine: escorting merchant convoys and policing duties, neither of which significantly tested Nelson or other sea officers. Despite twice suffering severely with his health during 16 years' service, what Nelson had fully learned was how to manage small ships' crews and maintain their health. More importantly, Nelson had gained an absolute understanding about the men who formed a ship's company: how they thought and how they worked. War with Revolutionary France six years later enabled him to draw on all his valuable experience.

## Nelson at war

Nelson was recalled and given command of HMS *Agamemnon* on 26 January 1793, sailing in June to join Lord Hood's Mediterranean squadron off Toulon. That October he saw action again and between January and August 1794 was involved in the Corsican campaign fighting in the sieges at Calvi and Bastia during which he lost the sight in his right eye. On 11 June 1796, Nelson took command of the 74-gun HMS *Captain*. Admiral Sir John Jervis then promoted him to commodore in command of a small, independent squadron deployed to cover the evacuation of Leghorn, Corsica and Elba as Bonaparte's armies marched through Italy.

On 19 August 1796, Spain allied herself to France and the British fleet withdrew from the Mediterranean. On 14 February 1797, Jervis's fleet went into action against a large Spanish squadron at the Battle of Cape St Vincent during which Nelson distinguished himself, though in an impulsive and foolhardy fashion. First, he disobeyed orders and swung his ship out of the rigid line of battle to prevent half of the Spanish ships from escaping. Second, he led from the front, boarding and capturing one ship, then boarding from this vessel to capture another, the entire act showing daring and quick thinking. Nelson appeared to be blindly gambling his career; failure would have seen him court-martialed. Instead he was knighted, promoted to rear-admiral and granted the Freedom of the City of London. His actions also brought Jervis an earldom.

In May 1797 Nelson hoisted his flag in HMS *Theseus*. That July he was again leading from the front and involved with hand-to-hand fighting in boat actions off Cadiz. His luck turned when he was sent on an expedition to Tenerife. During his planned the attack on Santa Cruz on 24 July, he lost his right arm during the amphibious assault. In all, his entire undertaking proved a total failure; he had completely misjudged the situation and the magnificent defense put up by General Gutiérrez. Sent home that September, he spent six months convalescing in Bath and London, facing possible retirement.

Determined to fight for his country Nelson again hoisted his flag in HMS *Vanguard* on 14 March 1798, spending May to July pursuing the French fleet in the Mediterranean, the action culminating at the victorious Battle of the Nile in the bay of Abu Kir off Alexandria on 1 August 1798. Cunningly leading his ships between the landward shoal water and Admiral de Brueys' anchored French fleet, this is perhaps Nelson's greatest and most daring battle tactic, especially as his singular battle plan was not prepared in advance, Nelson trusting the captains of his ships to take the initiative as circumstance evolved; manoeuvring large ships under sail in confined shallow waters took nerve. The manner in which Nelson defeated the French squadron certainly unnerved the French Navy. Villeneuve, who had commanded the French rear division at the Nile, remembered the experience of Nelson's extreme tenacity when forced to face him again at Trafalgar seven years later.

## The Neapolitan court

Despite crushing the French Mediterranean fleet Nelson had been wounded again, this time in the head, the neurological effects of which appeared to impair his moral judgment. This became evident when he took his fleet into Naples where he spent much time in the Neapolitan court in the company of King Ferdinand IV, Queen Caroline, the British ambassador Sir William Hamilton and his wife Emma Lady Hamilton. On 6 November Nelson was made Baron Nile. But at the same time he had struck an inappropriately close liaison with Emma Hamilton. With the threat of Jacobin forces converging on Naples, Nelson took it upon himself to save the monarchy and, using his ships, evacuated the Royal family, the Hamiltons and the court entourage from Naples to Palermo, Sicily, in late December. On returning, Nelson found Naples in turmoil, the Neapolitan fleet supporting the Jacobin rebels. He then appeared to get embroiled politically, authorising the hanging of the Neapolitan Admiral Caracciolo. For his services to the Neapolitan court, King Ferdinand made Nelson Duke of Bronte and gave him an estate in Sicily.

Added to all this activity, Nelson uncharacteristically disobeyed orders from his superior Lord Keith to sail to Minorca but, when given HMS *Foudroyant* he sailed for Malta, taking the Hamiltons with him. During this voyage, Emma conceived Nelson's child. His next irrational act was to return to England overland from Livorno with the Hamiltons rather than by sea as ordered; the journey through Europe taking five months. Perhaps inevitably, Nelson's homecoming on 8 November 1800, was coldly received by his wife Fanny.

## Back in home waters

In January 1801 Nelson and Fanny parted company and on 29 January Emma's and Nelson's illegitimate daughter Horatia was born. Ignoring his status and the glory of the Nile, caricatures in the press publicly lampooned both Nelson and Emma.

Nelson next hoisted his flag in HMS *San Josef* which he had captured earlier at the Battle of Cape St Vincent. Transferring into HMS *St George*, Nelson joined Admiral Parker's fleet at Yarmouth and sailed for the Baltic to fight the Danes. Needing a ship of shallower draught he went into HMS *Elephant* in which he fought at the Battle of Copenhagen on 1 April 1801 Although his earlier knowledge of these waters proved strategically advantageous, Nelson again turned a 'blind eye' and ignored his superior's orders. However, astutely aware of the deadlock that ensued between the opponents, Nelson exercised great diplomacy in bringing the battle to a close to avoid further unnecessary deaths. After succeeding Parker as Commander-in-Chief of the Baltic fleet, Nelson returned to England and was given the command of the naval forces in the English Channel. Although deployed to attack Bonaparte's invasion headquarters at Boulogne, these attempts proved a failure.

That September, Nelson bought Merton Place and set up home with Emma. On 25 March 1802 the Treaty of Amiens ended hostilities between Britain and the French Republic. In April Sir William Hamilton died. Having given a total of 25 years of devoted service to Britain and the Royal Navy, Nelson welcomed the peace and looked forward to retirement with Emma; unfortunately fate and the Trafalgar campaign prevented this.

## National loss

When news of the glorious victory of Trafalgar and Nelson's death reached England on 6 November 1805 Britain was both overwhelmed and adversely moved by the death of her national hero. Epitomising the public mood, the Poet Laureate Robert Southey wrote, *'Men started at the intelligence and turned pale as if they had heard of the death of a dear friend.'* At one event at the Covent Garden theatre an extra line was added to the national song *Rule, Britannia,'* *'Rule, brave Britons, rule the main, Avenge the god-like hero slain.'* Prime Minister William Pitt attending the Lord Mayor's Banquet on 9 November addressed the assembly: *'England has been saved by her exertions; and will, as I trust, save Europe by her example.'*

## State funeral

In January 1806, Nelson was the second commoner to be given a grand state funeral, the first being Sir Isaac Newton in 1727. The coffin was set on an ornate funeral car designed to look like HMS *Victory*, complete with a figurehead and bedecked with Nelson's trophies. Besides an escort of soldiers, the funeral car was accompanied by Nelson's fellow officers, members of the *Victory's* crew and Greenwich naval pensioners. Vast numbers of people lined the streets to view the procession and stands had been built with tickets sold for the best seats along the route. Also watching the funeral from an upstairs window was Admiral Villeneuve who, although a prisoner of war had been granted parole to watch the procession.

The procession took so long that was it was getting dark when the funeral car with Nelson's body arrived at St Paul's Cathedral where a special lantern mounting 130 individual lamps was suspended inside the dome. After a long service Nelson's body was buried in the crypt of St Paul's. This was followed by five days of public ceremonies in Greenwich, the River Thames and throughout the streets of London, demonstrating the widespread affection in which the dead hero was held.

## In memoriam

As Britain's naval hero Nelson was portrayed in numerous pictures and sketches by the fashionable artists of the period. Added to this are the innumerable paintings, engravings and aquatints of his battles, most created posthumously, which symbolically epitomise Nelson as a fearless man of action. He was also commemorated via a series of grand monuments, the most famous of which is Nelson's Column in London's Trafalgar Square.

# – APPENDIX 1 –

# THE *VICTORY'S* SAILING QUALITIES

## THE OBSERVATIONS OF THE QUALITY
## OF HIS MAJESTY'S SHIP *VICTORY*

Her best Sailing Draft of Water when Victualled and Stored for Channel Service {*Afore 23 Ft. 2 Ins.*} or as much lighter (at the same Difference) as she is able to bear Sail being given this 26*th* Day of Nov*r* 1797 {*Abaft    24Ft. 0 Ins.*}

Her Lowest Gundeck Port will be above the surface of the Water 5 Ft. 6 Ins.

| | |
|---|---|
| In a Topgallant Gale | *Behaves well, runs between 7 and 8 knots* |
| In a Topsail Gale | *D° as above will run 6, 7 or 8 knots* |
| Query the 1*st* How she Steers, and how she Wears and Stays | *She steers remarkably well, Wears very quick, and Seldom miss Stays when any other Ship will St…* |
| Under her…{ Reeft Topsails | *Sails 4, 5 or 6 knots}*<br>*We have always found her to behave well in each Circumstance* |
| Courses | *Sails 2, 3 or 4 knots}* |
| And Query, Whether she will Stay under her Courses | *Never Tryed her* |
| 2nd. In each Circumstance above mentioned (in Sailing with Other Ships) in what Proportion she gathers to Windward, and in what proportion she forereaches, and in general her Proportions in leeway | *In Sailing with Other ships, She holds her Wind very well with them, and forereaches upon most, or all Ships of three decks we have been in Company with, She makes Leeway from ½ a point in pretty Smooth water and increases as the sea rises, to 4 or 5 points under her Courses in a Great sea.* |
| 3rd. How she proves in Sailing thro' all the variations of the Wind from its being two feet abaft the Beam, to  its Veering forward upon the Bowline in every Strength of Gale, especially if a stiff Gale and a Head sea, and how many Knots she runs in each Circumstance and how she carries her Helm | *With the Wind Large she Sails well, she does with the Wind Veering forward to being close haul'd and forereaches upon most ships, but in a head sea she seldom more that hold her own with then, and will run from 10 Or 11 knots Large to 4 to 3 knots Close haul'd on a head Sea. Carries her helm generally ½ a turn of the wheel or Something less aweather, but in a head sea at times a little alee.* |

| 4th. The most knots she runs before the Wind; and how she Rolls in a trough of Sea | 10 to 11 knots – Rolls Easy and Strains nothing |
|---|---|
| 5th. How she behaves in Lying To, or a Try, under a Mainsail, also under a Mizon balanc'd | Lays too well, Especially under storm staysails |
| 6th. What a Roader she is, and how she Careens | She Rides rather heavy on her anchor, never Careen'd her. |
| 7th. If upon Trial the best sailing Draft of water given as above should not prove to be so what is her best sailing Draft of Water {Afore {Abaft | Ft.  Ins.<br>The above have found to be the best<br>Ft.  Ins.<br>24   3<br>25   6 |
| 8th. What is her best Draft of water when victualled for six Months, and Stored for Foreign Service {Afore {Abaft | Ft.  Ins.<br>24   3<br>25   6 |
| 9th. What height is her lowest Gundeck-Port above the Surface of the Water | 4   0 |
| 10th. Trim of the Ship | 10 Inches by the Stern |
| 11th. How she stand under sails | She is thought to be a Stiff Ship; easily bought down - ascertain bearing and after that sufficiently Stiff |
| 12th. The Quantities of Iron and Shingle Ballast on Board | 257 Tons of Iron, and 200 tons of Shingle |
| 13th. How she stows her Provisions and water and What Quantity of the latter she carries with four to six Months provisions; also that Quantity of Shingle or Iron Ballast which may be put out when she is victualled for Six Months | She will stow Four Months Provisions in the aft {hold} but when Six Months is ordered the Great part of the Wet provisions are obliged to be put in the Main hold with four Months provisions; Will carry 380 tons of Water and Six Months 335 tons. Bread room will just stow six months bread loose |
| 14th. The Weight of the Provisions taken on Board, in Consequence of being stored for the above | Suppose 6 Months Provisions to be 300 tons |

*Not having received a plan of the hold from the former Master – the stowage of Iron and shingle* – Will. Cummings Cap.

GR

# – APPENDIX 2 –

# THE WATCHES, SHIP'S TIME AND DAILY ROUTINE AT SEA

At sea each day commenced at 12 o'clock noon when astronomical sightings were taken to determine the ship's position and it was from this time that the daily routine was divided into a seven-watch system, not to be confused with the larboard and starboard divisions of seamen. Each watch and its time span were as follows:

| Time period (standard time) | Time period (24-hour time) | Watch title | Origins of title |
|---|---|---|---|
| 12 noon to 4.00pm | 12.00 to 16.00 | Afternoon | Self explanatory |
| 4.00pm to 6.00pm | 16.00 to 18.00 | First Dog | Associated with Dog Star Sirius |
| 6.00pm to 8.00pm | 18.00 to 20.00 | Second Dog* | Associated with Dog Star Sirius |
| 8.00pm to 12 midnight | 20.00 to 23.59 | First | The first watch of the night |
| 12.00 midnight to 4.00am | 00.00 to 04.00 | Middle | The middle of the night |
| 4.00am to 8.00am | 04.00 to 08.00 | Morning | Self explanatory |
| 8.00am to 12 noon | 08.00 to 12.00 | Forenoon | Self explanatory |

Ship's time was notified by striking the ship's bell mounted in its belfry at the after end of the forecastle. Time was measured using an hour- and a half-hour sand glass, the timekeeper manning the bell ringing it every half-hour, the number of rings denoting actual time; taking the afternoon, First Dog and the First watches, for example, the bell was rung as follows with eight bells terminating the previous watch:

| Watch | Time | 24-hour time | No. of rings |
|---|---|---|---|
| Afternoon | 12.00 | 12.00 | 8 bells |
| | 12.30pm | 12.30 | 1 bell |
| | 1.00pm | 13.00 | 2 bells |
| | 1.30pm | 13.30 | 3 bells |
| | 2.00pm | 14.00 | 4 bells |
| | 2.30pm | 14.30 | 5 bells |
| | 3.00pm | 15.00 | 6 bells |
| | 3.30pm | 15.30 | 7 bells |
| First Dog | 4.00pm | 16.00 | 8 bells |
| | 4.30pm | 16.30 | 1 bell |
| | 5.00pm | 17.00 | 2 bells |
| | 5.30pm | 17.30 | 3 bells |
| Second (or Last) Dog | 6.00pm | 18.00 | 8 bells |
| | 6.30pm | 18.30 | 1 bell |
| | 7.00pm | 19.00 | 2 bells |
| | 7.30pm | 19.30 | 3 bells |
| First | 8.00pm | 20.00 | 8 bells |
| | 8.30pm | 20.30 | 1 bells |
| | 9.00pm | 21.00 | 2 bells |
| | 9.30pm | 21.30 | 3 bells |
| | 10.00pm | 22.00 | 4 bells |
| | 10.30pm | 22.30 | 5 bells |
| | 11.00pm | 23.00 | 6 bells |
| | 11.30pm | 23.30 | 7 bells |
| Middle | 12.00am | 00.00 | 8 bells |

## Allocation of manpower at quarters

| Lower gun deck: thirty 32-pounders | | Poop deck | |
|---|---|---|---|
| Second lieutenant | 1 | Fifth lieutenant | 1 |
| Sixth lieutenant | 1 | Captain of marines | 1 |
| Midshipmen | 4 | First lieutenant of marines | 1 |
| Mates | 2 | Second lieutenant of marines | 1 |
| Quarter gunners | 4 | Third lieutenant of marines | 1 |
| Gun captains – one per two guns | 15 | Sergeant of marines | 1 |
| Gun crew – 14 per two guns | 195 | Marines | 8 |
| **Total** | **222** | **Total** | **14** |
| **Middle gun deck: twenty-eight 24-pounders** | | **For signals on quarterdeck and poop deck** | |
| Third lieutenant | 1 | Midshipmen | 3 |
| Seventh lieutenant | 1 | Clerks | 3 |
| Midshipmen | 4 | Mates | 1 |
| Mates | 1 | Seamen | 6 |
| Quarter gunners | 4 | **Total** | **13** |
| Gun captains – one per two guns | 14 | **Aloft** | |
| Gun crew – 14 per two guns | 154 | Captain of the fore top | 1 |
| **Total** | **179** | Foretop men | 3 |
| **Upper gun deck: thirty 12-pounders** | | Captain of the main top | 2 |
| Fourth lieutenant | 1 | Mizzen top men | 2 |
| Eighth lieutenant | 1 | Boatswain's mates and seamen for rigging | 14 |
| Midshipmen | 4 | **Total** | **22** |
| Mates | 1 | **Magazines and handling powder** | |
| Quarter gunners | 4 | Grand magazine: gunner | 1 |
| Gun captains – one per two guns | 15 | Grand magazine: gunner's mates | 4 |
| Gun crew – 14 per two guns | 135 | Grand magazine: cooper | 1 |
| **Total** | **161** | Light rooms: master-at-arms | 1 |

| Quarterdeck: twelve 12-pounders | | Light rooms: cook and supply | 2 |
|---|---|---|---|
| Captain | 1 | After hanging magazine: yeoman | 1 |
| Master | 1 | After hanging magazine: landsmen | 2 |
| First lieutenant | 1 | Fore hatchway: landsmen and boys | 17 |
| Midshipmen | 4 | Main hatchway: landsmen and boys | 23 |
| Aides de camp and clerks | 3 | After hatchway: landsmen and boys | 26 |
| Quartermaster | 1 | Total | 81 |
| Quartermaster's mates | 5 | Orlop: cockpit, well, wings and store rooms | |
| Gun crew – 14 per two guns | 6 | Surgeon | 1 |
| Gun crew – nine per two guns | 54 | Assistant surgeon | 1 |
| Total | 76 | Surgeon's assistants and loblolly boys | 5 |
| Forecastle: two 12-pounder guns and two 68-pounder carronades | | Purser | 1 |
| Ninth lieutenant | 1 | Chaplain | 1 |
| Boatswain | 1 | Carpenter's and boatswain's store rooms | 2 |
| Midshipmen | 2 | Gunner's and purser's store rooms | 2 |
| Mates | 1 | Well and wings: carpenter | 1 |
| Gun captain – one per two 12-pounder guns | 1 | Carpenter's mates and crew | 14 |
| Gun crew – nine per two 12-pounder guns | 9 | Total | 28 |
| Gun crew – eight per two carronades | 8 | Grand total | 820 |
| Total | 24 | | |

# – APPENDIX 3 –

# QUANTITY OF SHOT AND GUNPOWDER EXPENDED AT THE BATTLE OF TRAFALGAR

| Table 1 Solid round shot | | | | | |
|---|---|---|---|---|---|
| | Quantity | Weight (Imperial) | | Weight (metric) | |
| Size | Rounds | lb | tons | kg | tonnes |
| 32lb | 997 | 31, 904 | 14.24 | 14,460 | 14.46 |
| 24lb | 872 | 20,028 | 9.34 | 94,490 | 9.49 |
| 12lb | 800 | 9600 | 4.29 | 4360 | 4.36 |
| **Total** | **26,659** | **62,432** | **27.87** | **28,320** | **28.32** |

| Table 2 Additional miscellaneous shot | | | | | | |
|---|---|---|---|---|---|---|
| | Type and no. of rounds | | Weight (Imperial) | | Weight (metric) | |
| Size | Double-headed | Grape | lb | tons | kg | tonnes |
| 32lb | 10 | 10 | 640 | 0.29 | 290 | 0.29 |
| 24lb | 11 | 20 | 744 | 0.33 | 340 | 0.34 |
| 12lb | 14 | 156 | 2040 | 0.91 | 920 | 0.92 |
| **Total** | **35** | **186** | **3424** | **1.53** | **1550** | **1.55** |

| Table 3 Quantity of gunpowder expended | | | |
|---|---|---|---|
| Weight (imperial) | | Weight (metric) | |
| lb | tons | kg | tonnes |
| 17,100 | 7.634 | 7800 | 7.8 |

# – APPENDIX 4 –

# *VICTORY'S* BATTLE CASUALTIES KILLED IN ACTION

1. French Revolutionary War: Siege of Calvi, 1 August 1794

| Rank/Rate | Name |
|---|---|
| Able Seaman | John Brown |
| Able Seaman | Alexander Brown |
| Able Seaman | George Jackson |

2. French Revolutionary War: Battle of Hyères Islands 13 July 1795

| Rank/Rate | Name |
|---|---|
| Midshipman | James Beale |
| Midshipman | John Willison |
| Marine Sergeant | Thomas Hands |
| Marine Private | John Harding |
| Marine Private | John Ryan |

3. Anglo-Spanish War: Battle of Cape St Vincent, 14 February 1797

| Rank/Rate | Name |
|---|---|
| Ordinary Seaman | Anthony Gramoda (Italian) |
| Marine Private | Thomas Keen |

4. Napoleonic War: Battle of Cape Trafalgar 21 October 1805

| Table 1 Officers and other ranks | | |
|---|---|---|
| | Rank/Rate | Name |
| 1 | Vice-Admiral | Horatio Lord Nelson |
| 2 | Captain of Marines | Charles Adair |
| 3 | Lieutenant | William Ram |
| 4 | Midshipman | Alexander Palmer |
| 5 | Midshipman | Robert Smith |

| 6 | Secretary | John Scott |
| 7 | Captain's Clerk | Thomas Whipple |
| 8 | Petty Officer Quarter Master | John King |
| 9 | Petty Officer Quarter Gunner | Thomas Johnson |
| 10 | Petty Officer Carpenter's Crew | George Laing |

| Table 2 Seamen | | |
|---|---|---|
| 1 | Able Seaman | William Brown |
| 2 | Able Seaman | Robert Davidson |
| 3 | Able Seaman | Joseph Gordon |
| 4 | Able Seaman | James Mansell |
| 5 | Able Seaman | William Muck |
| 6 | Able Seaman | Alfred Taylor |
| 7 | Able Seaman | William Thompson |
| 8 | Able Seaman | John Walker |
| 9 | Able Seaman | Edward Waters |
| 10 | Ordinary Seaman | Jonathan Corwarder |
| 11 | Ordinary Seaman | Charles Davis |
| 12 | Ordinary Seaman | Arthur Herwin |
| 13 | Ordinary Seaman | Richard Jewel |
| 14 | Ordinary Seaman | James North |
| 15 | Ordinary Seaman | James Park |
| 16 | Ordinary Seaman | William Onions |
| 17 | Ordinary Seaman | William Shinner |
| 18 | Ordinary Seaman | James Skinner |
| 19 | Ordinary Seaman | William Smith |
| 20 | Ordinary Seaman | Robert Thompson |
| 21 | Ordinary Seaman | Josiah Ward |
| 22 | Ordinary Seaman | John Wharton |

| 23 | Landsman | John Bowler |
|----|----------|-------------|
| 24 | Landsman | William Cale |
| 25 | Landsman | Henry Cramwell |
| 26 | Landsman | Thomas Daniels |
| 27 | Landsman | William Shaw |
| 28 | Landsman | George Smith |
| 29 | Boy | James McPherson |
| 30 | Boy | Colin Turner |
| 31 | Boy | George Wilson |

| Table 3 Royal Marines | | |
|----|----------|-------------|
| 1 | Marine Corporal | George Cockran |
| 2 | Marine Drummer | James Berry |
| 3 | Marine Private | John Brennan |
| 4 | Marine Private | John Brown |
| 5 | Marine Private | John Edsworth |
| 6 | Marine Private | James Green |
| 7 | Marine Private | Daniel Hillier |
| 8 | Marine Private | William Jones |
| 9 | Marine Private | George Kennedy |
| 10 | Marine Private | Jeremiah Lewis |
| 11 | Marine Private | Bernard McManus |
| 12 | Marine Private | Lamberd Myers |
| 13 | Marine Private | James Norgrove |
| 14 | Marine Private | John Palmer |
| 15 | Marine Private | William Perry |
| 16 | Marine Private | George Willmott |
| 17 | Marine Private | Samuel Wilkes |

# ‑ PRIMARY SOURCES ‑

His Majesty in Council. *Regulations and Instructions Relating to His Majesty's Service at Sea 1808*.

Signal book of HMS *Dreadnought* 1805.

National Maritime Museum (NMM).*Victory: Lines as Built 1759*. No. 205 box 4 ZAZ. 0122.

NMM. Victory: Profile off inboard works No. 206 B box 4 ZAZ. 0122. & PS 40/01 HM. Dockyard Portsmouth.

National Archive (NA). ADM. 180/10. Progress Book (HMS *Victory*).

NA. ADM. 95/39. Observations of the Sailing Qualities of His Majesty's Ship *Victory* 1797.

NA. ADM 51 Series: Captain's Log books.

NA. ADM 52 Series: Master's Log books.

NA. ADM 160 Series: Ship's Ordnance Records.

NA. WO 44 Series: War Office Records (ordnance).

National Royal Navy Museum (NRNM). MSS 1998/41 River's Papers. Journals of Master Gunner William Rivers in HMS *Victory* 1793–1811.

NRNM. MSS 1986/573. (11) River's Papers. Journals of Midshipman William Rivers in HMS *Victory*.

NRNM. MSS 1064/ 83. 2376, Record of Carpenters and Boatswains Stores and Expenses for HM Ships Victory, Britannia and Africa for year 1805 (covers July to December 1805).

NRNM. MSS118. Order book of Captain John Sutton HMS Egmont 1798 – 1801 and HMS Superb 1798 – 1801.

HMS Victory Archive. (VA) VLDA.2000. Letters and Document Archive.

VA. VPA2000. Photographic Archive.

## PRIMARY PUBLISHED

Anon. *The Shipbuilders Repository* London 1789.

Jackson, T.S. *Logs of the Great Sea Fights 1794–1803*. Vol.1. NRS. No 16 1899.

Lavery, B. *Shipboard Life and Organisation 1731–1815*. NRS. No 138. London. 1998.

Morris, R. The Chanel Fleet and Blockade of Brest 1793–1801. NRS. No 141 London. 2001.

Rudyard, C.W. *Course of Artillery*. London 1793.

Steel D. *Elements of Mastmaking, Sailmaking and Rigging*. London 1794.

Steel D. *Elements and Practice of Naval Architecture*. London 1804.

Tracy, N. (ed) *The Naval Chronicle: The Contemporary Record of the Royal Navy at War*, 5 vols (London 1999 consolidated edition).

# – INDEX –